Queering the Museum

Queering the Museum develops a queer analysis of the ways in which museums construct themselves, their core business, and their publics through the, often unconscious, use of inherited ways of knowing and doing.

Providing a critique of both the practices and conventions associated with the modern public museum, and the ontological assumptions that inform them, the authors consider recent discourse around inclusion in museums and explore the ways this has been taken up in practice. Highlighting the limits of particular approaches to inclusion, and the failure to move away from a traditional museological paradigm, the book outlines an alternative critical museological approach that the authors refer to as 'queer'. Providing readers with the critical tools necessary for a profound rethinking of museum practice, the book also responds to and problematises the growing call for social inclusion.

Queering the Museum will appeal to academics, students, and museum and arts sector practitioners with an interest in critical theory or queer practice. It will be of particular interest to those working in the fields of museum studies, sociology, archaeology, anthropology, cultural studies, media, social policy, politics, philosophy, and history.

Nikki Sullivan is Manager of the Centre of Democracy in Adelaide, South Australia. She is also Adjunct Associate Professor in the School of Humanities, Faculty of Arts, University of Adelaide.

Craig Middleton is Curator at the National Museum of Australia, Canberra. His research and practice explore political histories and histories of activism, LGBTIQ+ histories, and critical museology.

Museums in Focus

Series Editor: Kylie Message

Australian National University, Australia

Committed to the articulation of big, even risky ideas, in small format publications, 'Museums in Focus' challenges authors and readers to experiment with, innovate, and press museums and the intellectual frameworks through which we view these. It offers a platform for approaches that radically rethink the relationships between cultural and intellectual dissent and crisis and debates about museums, politics and the broader public sphere.

'Museums in Focus' is motivated by the intellectual hypothesis that museums are not innately 'useful', 'safe' or even 'public' places, and that recalibrating our thinking about them might benefit from adopting a more radical and oppositional form of logic and approach. Examining this problem requires a level of comfort with (or at least tolerance of) the idea of crisis, dissent, protest and radical thinking, and authors might benefit from considering how cultural and intellectual crisis, regeneration and anxiety have been dealt with in other disciplines and contexts.

Museums, Infinity and the Culture of Protocols
Ethnographic Collections and Source Communities
Howard Morphy

Anti-Museum
Adrian Franklin

Queering the Museum
Nikki Sullivan and Craig Middleton

www.routledge.com/Museums-in-Focus/book-series/MIF

MUSEUMS IN FOCUS

Logo by James Verdon (2017)

Queering the Museum

Nikki Sullivan and Craig Middleton

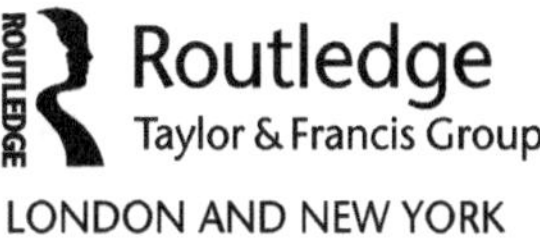

LONDON AND NEW YORK

First published 2020
by Routledge
2 Park Square, Milton Park, Abingdon, Oxon OX14 4RN

and by Routledge
605 Third Avenue, New York, NY 10017

First issued in paperback 2021

Routledge is an imprint of the Taylor & Francis Group, an informa business

Publisher's Note
The publisher has gone to great lengths to ensure the quality of this reprint but points out that some imperfections in the original copies may be apparent.

British Library Cataloguing-in-Publication Data
A catalogue record for this book is available from the British Library

Library of Congress Cataloging-in-Publication Data
Library of Congress Control Number: 2019949887

ISBN 13: 978-1-03-208594-4 (pbk)
ISBN 13: 978-0-815-35962-3 (hbk)

Typeset in Times New Roman
by Apex CoVantage, LLC

Contents

Figures

Acknowledgements

Many individuals and groups have supported us in the development of this book.

We want to thank the following people and groups for their participation in two of our own projects which we have discussed in the book: Barbara Baird, Charlotte Coulthard-Dare, Dane Wilden, Em König, Jackie Wurm, Jenny Scott, Marc der Veer, Richard Boyle, Troy-Anthony Baylis, Vicki Rich, Feast Queer Youth Drop-in and Southern Youth Rainbow Space, Margie Fischer, and Natrydd Sigurthur.

We want to thank the following people who generously shared their work and ideas with us and/or gave permission for us to include them here: Charlotte Keenan McDonald, David Fleming, Jo Darbyshire, Matt Smith, Richard Sandell, Kellie Greene, and Vika Kirchenbauer.

We want to thank Mandy Paul and Allison Russell for being critical friends, reading drafts, and offering insightful feedback on the manuscript, and also the anonymous readers whose comments on our proposal helped clarify our vision.

Finally, we would like to thank our partners, Kellie and Malakai, and our families for their ongoing support for our queer mission.

Introduction

Queering the Museum takes as its starting point three claims commonly found in contemporary museological literature. The first is that museums are both shaped by and shape the socio-political landscapes in which they operate and are thus implicated in systems of power and privilege (Bennett, 1995; Hooper-Greenhill, 1992; Sherman & Rogoff, 1994). The second is that despite growing sectoral concerns around inclusion, lesbian, gay, bisexual, transgender, intersex, and queer (LGBTIQ+) his/stories, lives, identities, and issues continue to be largely absent in museums internationally (McIntyre, 2007; Vanegas, 2010; Mulhearn, 2015; Sandell, 2017), and this has very real material effects for LGBTIQ+-identified people and their allies (Heimlich & Koke, 2008; Conlan, 2010).[1] The third is that museums can, and we contend, should, be active participants in the articulation of critically engaged and socially transformative ways of seeing, knowing, being, doing. Moving beyond the kinds of approaches offered by social inclusion and/or human rights frameworks, *Queering the Museum* elaborates a 'queering' of contemporary museum practices, the often invisiblised assumptions that inform them, and the social and political effects they produce. As an intervention aimed at problematising the dominant, heteronormative, museological paradigms and the policies, practices, and subject positions to which they give rise, *Queering the Museum* at once engages with the struggles museums have had around the question of ethics, and performatively invokes an alternative understanding of ethics as critical practice.

Talking terms

So, what do we mean when, in the title of the book, we refer to 'the museum'? In using this term we do not mean to imply the existence of a singular, monolithic, unchanging entity. Indeed, it goes without saying that museums are many and varied, and while some – maybe even most – share some ideas about their purpose and function, or some ways of doing some things, each is nevertheless uniquely situated. Museums have different disciplinary histories that shape their identities and their practices: art museums have different remits, aims and objectives, values and approaches to natural history museums; science museums have different collections, foci, taxonomies, and ways of understanding than social history museums. Additionally, historic/heritage sites, botanical gardens, arboretums, aquariums, zoos, and so on are all museums of a particular kind – some have static collections, others have living collections. Increasingly we are seeing an emergence of museums without walls, challenging the bricks and mortar notion of what a museum is. The Museum of Homelessness, The Museum of Transology, and the Museum of Water are examples of this.

Just as museums are diverse, so too is their administration. The most fundamental difference at the level of governance is between museums that are publicly funded (wholly or in part) by governments and local authorities and those that are funded privately (wholly or in part) by benefactors, foundations, charitable originations (for example the National Trust, Historic Royal Palaces, and so on), and corporations (such as banks). Publicly funded museums may be overseen by ministries as diverse as education, tourism, defence, environment, national heritage, and arts, and the level and type of state control varies from county to country. (Lewis, 2019:npn). Despite the differences between them, publicly funded institutions are generally more highly regulated, more risk-averse, and have less freedom to experiment than those that are privately funded. Nowhere is this clearer than in the case of Hobart's Museum of Old and New Art (MONA), which when it opened in 2011 was alleged to be the largest privately funded museum in the southern hemisphere.[2] Owner and founder of MONA, David Walsh, who made his fortune through professional gambling, seems neither constrained by, nor interested in, the idea(l)s, mores, conventions, and codes of ethics that govern publicly funded art institutions. Indeed, he actively courts controversy.

More interesting to us (at least in the context of the point we wish to make here) than the housing of exhibitions that have caused a public outcry and/or been rejected by other art museums[3] is Walsh's selling of a work by Damien Hirst from MONA's collection in order "to make MORE MONA – another wing to house his James Turrell fetish" (Pearce, 2015). If the Tasmanian Museum and Art Gallery, Tasmania's publicly funded museum and gallery, were to sell one of the works from its collection to support capital development, the public scrutiny, political ramifications, and reputational damage would be significant. What this suggests is that how a museum is funded and thus governed fundamentally effects its operations, its identity, its position, and its purpose.[4]

When we speak of 'the museum', then, we speak not of a singular entity, but of an abstract idea(l) that shapes, but does not wholly define, the various institutions – both concrete and virtual – that we call museums. A highly influential example of this idea(l) can be found in the definition offered in the International Council of Museums (ICOM) Statutes 2007, which reads,

> a museum is a nonprofit, permanent institution, in the service of society and of its development, open to the public, which acquires, conserves, researches, communicates, and exhibits the tangible and intangible heritage of humanity and its environment for the purposes of education, study and enjoyment.[5]

Interestingly, ICOM has recently acknowledged that the last couple of decades has witnessed the radical transformation of museums to the point that this definition no longer seems to accurately reflect what museums are and do.[6] Consequently, the organisation has invited members and other interested parties to contribute to the creation of a new and more relevant definition. However, while on the one hand ICOM's claim that "a new definition can be terse as law or concise as a poem" suggests a level of openness to new and innovative ways of knowing, doing, and being, on the other, the list of eight "parameters" that contributors are advised should be contained or reflected in their suggested definitions are indicative of the organisation's ongoing conservatism. The latter is most clear in the first (and thus presumably the most significant) parameter which reads, "The museum definition should retain – even if current terminology may vary – the *unique, defining, and essential unity* in museums of the functions of collecting, preserving, documenting, researching, exhibiting and in other ways communicating the collections or other evidence of cultural heritage" (emphasis in the original).

Circumscribing new definitions in this way is highly problematic for reasons that will become apparent as the book unfolds, but for now it is worth noting that what this, and the other parameters listed in the call for contributions, makes clear is that the identity of 'the museum' is both shaped by, and shapes, its function and purpose: it lies not in what it *is* (in any essential sense) but in what it *does*, why, and how. According to Mark O'Neill (2006), idea(l)s about the purpose and function of museums can be loosely associated with three views which he calls essentialist, adaptive, and ideological. These three perspectives, he notes, are held "to varying degrees by staff and board members within individual museums. . . . [M]useums, both in their own terms and in terms of their place in society, are fragmented and not wholly coherent institutions" (2006:98). O'Neill's claim is integral to the analyses we offer throughout the book: it reminds us to avoid conceiving museums and museological practice in binary terms – good/bad, us/them/, progressive/anachronistic, inclusive/exclusory – and enables us to queer ways of knowing, doing, and being that deny complexity, connection, and open-endedness.

Those who subscribe to the essentialist view – as ICOM appears to – conceive the museum as an institution whose primary function is to collect, preserve, research, and display objects, and whose identity is consequently fundamentally unchanging.[7] The museum, on this model, is a sort of neutral, objective medium, a "clean, clear, and undistorting lens" through which visitors can encounter the "thing-in-itself" (Weil, 1994:80–81). Drawing, in part, on interviews conducted by Peter Falconer with senior staff in national museums and galleries in London and Edinburgh, O'Neill argues that many of those who work in museums that view themselves in this way feel that they are "part of a beleaguered minority, defending cultural heritage and the arts against a new breed of philistines"[8] whose focus on social justice and wider access is "inimical to the nature of museums" (2006:96–97). This position is exemplified by Josie Appleton's claim that the traditional functions of the art museum – that is, presenting and interpreting great works of art, and valuing them for the inspiration they can provide – are undervalued in "today's cultural policy circles". The use of scarce resources to develop "feely boxes", interactives that allow visitors to manipulate their facial features, and protective coatings for modern sculptures so that they be touched without being damaged,[9] is, Appleton argues, evidence of the extent to which museums' "priorities have become distorted" (2002:npn); to the fact that the value of collections is no longer seen to reside in the collection itself, but rather, is (mis)understood in terms of social ends.

What O'Neill identifies as the adaptive view of the museum is founded on the assumption that museums must, first and foremost, serve their publics, and that, in order to do so, they must adapt with and to the social context in which they operate. While the need to be adaptive is nothing new since, as Hooper-Greenhill explains, "museums have always had to modify how they worked, and what they did, according to the context, the plays of power, and the social, economic, and political imperatives that surrounded them" (1992:1), the dominant vision of the museum as "socially purposeful" (Museums Association, 2017:3), and informed by a social justice agenda, is specific to the here and now, as we explain in Chapter 1. Proponents of this model foreground the museum's activist role – arguing that museums can and should work to counter social injustice (poverty, inequality, intolerance, discrimination, and so on), inspire engagement, debate, and reflection, and contribute to social cohesion, health, and wellbeing. They tend, suggests O'Neill, to "see themselves as reformers" (2006:97)[10] working against exclusionary beliefs and practices within their own institutions and/or within the sector as a whole.

On this model the collection, preservation, and display of objects is less an end in itself, than one means by which museums might fulfil their (presumed) civic responsibilities; thus museums without collections – of which there are an increasing number – are not, as they would be on the essentialist model, understood as a contradiction in terms. Moreover, if as Weil argues, the museum should be understood not as an end in itself, but as a starting point "for a process intended to continue long after the visitor has left the museum's premises" (1994:84), then museums are less places bounded by walls, than technologies[11] (Bennett, 2005) that contribute to world-making. Hooper-Greenhill (2000) uses the term 'post-museum' to refer to this enlarged and politicised (post-modern) scope and mission. Taking this argument one step further, Dewdney, Dibosa, and Walsh suggest that 'the museum' consists of a set of intersecting local and distributed networks that extend an institution's walls, beyond national boundaries, and are in constant flux.[12] In regard to art museums, they argue, such networks include

> the permanent civil service, art markets, the professional art world, cultural practitioners, dimensions of broadcast and publishing media and others. In these networks, people and things, such as the objects of collection, ideas and policies, are all active elements, with varying degrees of agency in determining what a particular network does and doesn't do.
>
> (2012:118)

From this perspective, the museum is not just an institution, a place, but also a set of practices that cannot be separated out from the contexts in which they operate: the museum as a doing (verb) as much as a thing (noun).

In different ways, and to varying degrees, both the essentialist and adaptive views of the museum could, we suggest, be said to support hegemonic[13] structures of power and knowledge, and the inequalities they give rise to. In the contemporary museological context this critique of the essentialist view of the museum is relatively uncontentious: the modernist museum is widely conceived as an "anti-democratic, elitist, patriarchal, [heteronormative], colonizing instrument of class and imperial oppression" (O'Neill, 2006:98). It is, however, much less common to find this kind of criticism levelled at the adaptive view of the museum, framed as it currently is in terms of inclusion, equality, human rights, social justice, and so on. But if museum professionals are genuinely committed to radically changing museums in order to make them more relevant to larger numbers of people, and to ensure that they play an active role in social change, then we need to acknowledge that we still have an extremely long way to go, that, despite all our efforts at inclusion to date, research shows that the majority of museum visitors continue to be white, middle-upper class, well-educated, and so on.[14] And, we contend, we need to pay more critical attention to the ways in which implicit, but nevertheless structural and structuring idea(l)s, shape museums and the identities and actions of those who compose them. This is the aim of *Queering the Museum*.

Motivations, scope, limits, and approach

The queering of museums is, as we understand it, a process without end, and, perhaps more importantly, without a definitive goal (for example, social inclusion) that is presumed to be universally beneficial and achievable by following a particular path. As the progeny of poststructuralism, queer/ing necessarily eschews singular certainties. *Queering the Museum*, then, should be viewed not as a blueprint, a game plan for a brave new (queer) world of museums and museological practice, but rather as a (necessarily incomplete) toolbox that can be used, expanded, and adapted in ways that are, perhaps, currently unimaginable.

Our motivation for writing the book stems primarily from a feeling of frustration with regard to the scholarship on museums and museological practice that is available to practitioners. One the one hand, the last three decades or so has seen a deluge of academic scholarship in this area, and yet, from our perspective, much of it fails to really engage with or impact on the day-to-day realities of working in the sector. This is not to suggest that such work is not important or useful, indeed, *Queering the Museum* is heavily influenced by museological scholarship. On the other hand, when museum professionals publish accounts of exhibitions and the like these are often largely descriptive and lack the kind of critical self-reflection and theoretical analysis that we contend is necessary if radical change is to occur. In short, there seems to us to be a gap between theory and practice, between the work that is carried out in universities and the work that is carried out in museums. All too often "the museum is posited as the concrete operational sphere considered as the object of abstract reflection by the academy" (Dewdney et al., 2013:221), just as theory is regularly dismissed by museum professionals as something that academics do, and that museum staff are either uninterested in, or simply don't have time for.[15] For us, divisions such as these – and the material effects they produce – are problematic and in need of queering. The work of tackling and of troubling (both conceptually and operationally) what museums do, how, and why, needs, we argue, to take place "in and with museums and their extended collaborators in a reflexive methodological mode" (Dewdney et al., 2013:224). This is how we understand our own museological practice: as situated at the intersection of theory and practice, and thus, as praxis.

Like all museum professionals, our practice and our positions are shaped by the context in which we currently work as well as by our professional and personal histories. When writing this book we were both employed by the History Trust of South Australia (HTSA), a statutory authority that was established by an Act of the South Australian Parliament in 1981 to carry out a number of roles and activities, including managing the Migration Museum, the National Motor Museum, the South Australian Maritime Museum, and, more recently, the Centre of Democracy.[16] Because, unlike other Australian states, South Australia does not have a museum dedicated to the state's history, the Migration Museum cares for the State History Collection (as well as the Migration Collection). The HTSA's (social history) museums are largely government funded, and report to a Board of Trustees appointed by the Governor of South Australia, and to the South Australian Parliament through the Minister for Education.

One of us (Nikki) is a curator at the Migration Museum, a small institution with approximately 14 employees, a third of whom are on fractional appointments. The other (Craig) is the manager, curator, and only full-time staff member of the Centre of Democracy. The size of our organisations means that our roles are many and varied: we both curate exhibitions; carry out research for in-house projects; are involved in collections management; develop, manage, and implement public programmes; lead tours; contribute to our organisation's social media presence; develop and maintain partnerships; represent our institutions at conferences nationally and internationally; engage with communities; contribute to policy development; train arts sector employees in LGBTIQ+ inclusion; and publish our own research. As such, our experience of museum practice is presumably quite different to those who work in large institutions and whose roles may be more circumscribed and distinct.

Our careers to date have meant that we bring particular ways of seeing, knowing, and doing to the work we are currently engaged in. Craig's academic training is in Museum Studies and Art History, with a focus more latterly on political history and public participation. Prior to taking up his current position Craig's employment in the GLAM sector has consisted primarily of audience-facing and -focused roles in public programmes, marketing, and community partnerships. This professional trajectory has drawn on and contributed to a long-term commitment to critical engagement and activism that cannot be separated from his subject position as queer-identified. Prior to becoming a curator at the Migration Museum in 2015, Nikki spent over 20 years in academia where she trained in Gender and Cultural Studies and taught and published widely on, amongst other things, queer theory. As a queer-identified cisgender woman with a long-standing commitment to queering heteronormative epistemologies, practices, and the relations between them, she is constantly surprised by the extent to which museums fail to actively engage with sexuality, sex, and gender, and, in doing so, reaffirm knowledges and practices that privilege heteronormative power relations. From the poststructuralist perspective she inhabits, radically changing museums requires museum professionals to critically interrogate not only what we know and do, but also *how* we know and do. *Queering the Museum* provides tools that enable practitioners to undertake this kind of theoretically informed work, and in doing so contributes to the bridging of the theory/practice divide. It offers readers insights into how their work in museums can (and does) contribute to the co-production of knowledge, identity, and systems of power and privilege, and thus to world-making. It is our hope, as we make clear throughout the book, that the near future will see more work published by practitioners that engages, in theoretically informed ways, with the work they do, the context(s) in which it is carried out, the constraints and affordances that shape its articulation, and the effects it produces.

The approach we employ has two aims. First, given that *Queering the Museum* is the first monograph focussing on queering[17] to be written by practitioners wholly employed in museums, and is primarily targeted at museum staff and students, we aim to provide a survey – necessarily inexhaustive – of some of the work that has been published on the various aspects of practice that we discuss. As an introduction to the work of theorists (of both museology and other disciplines) whose ideas have most influenced us, *Queering the Museum* furnishes readers with a starting point from which to carry out further research, to pursue matters that are pertinent to them and their situation. Second, we develop detailed analyses of examples of work that, for us, queers traditional museological idea(l)s and practices. The examples selected for inclusion are by no means the only examples of such work, nor are they necessarily more successful (however that might be defined) than others – in fact our aim is not to definitively proclaim the queerness (or lack thereof) of particular projects. Our choices about what to include have largely been shaped by our knowledge of a specific project or elements thereof: we have chosen to discuss only projects that we have been involved in, or that had been undertaken by colleagues with whom we were able to confer,[18] or that we could access substantial documentation about.[19] We have avoided engaging with projects about which we only have superficial knowledge because, as we explain in Chapter 4, it is highly problematic to evaluate a project without having an in-depth understanding of the mechanics of production, that is, the often invisible constraints and affordances particular to a given context that shape the decisions made, the final product, and its relationship to other projects and to the institution's remit and its ongoing plans and relations.

Our focus on specific projects should not be taken to suggest that we regard such projects as wholly queer (whatever that might mean) or that every aspect of the project is equally pertinent to the aims of the book. Projects of all kinds, we suggest, are never singular, coherent, or clearly bounded, but rather necessarily involve complex and contradictory elements and outcomes, and are inextricable from the contexts in which they occur. As such, it is often specific aspects of a project that are illustrative of particular ideas rather than the project as a whole. However, since most undertakings involve multiple agents whose positions in relation to a project are diverse, interpretations, evaluations, and experiences will vary: what one person interprets as queering normative idea(l)s may appear to another person to be problematic. In other words, all interpretations, we contend, are situated and reflect the position, perspective, commitments, concerns, and so on of the person who interprets rather than being an accurate, objective description or evaluation of the thing interpreted. Consequently, it would be a mistake to think that an approach or tactic deployed in one situation can simply be applied in others without consideration of the context, the parties involved, and so on.

While the aim of the critiques we elaborate is to open up the rationalities that govern museological ways of knowing, being, and doing to queering, the book should not be understood as offering the definitive answer to the problem of heteronormativity in museums. We want to make clear from the outset that we are not suggesting that the approaches to queering discussed in this book should replace all other approaches, but rather that the kinds of interventions we explore can be used in combination with a range of other techniques, including more traditional ones. As we explain in the following chapters, insofar as museums vary widely in their remits, contexts, compositions, histories, limits, and affordances, museum practitioners must necessarily develop strategic interventions pertinent to their own particular situations and concerns. In short, different projects, undertaken in different contexts, will require different tools, techniques, approaches, and combinations thereof. For us it is the intersecting, often contradictory nature of multiple approaches employed by museums that enhance their ability to participate in critical self-reflection and achieve previously unimaginable outcomes. Our hope is that *Queering Museum* will challenge our readers' understanding of museological practice and open up discussion about the potential of alternative approaches: that it will furnish readers with a range of flexible tools and insights that can be adopted, adapted, expanded, and critiqued in the service of radically and persistently pursued institutional change.

The structure of the book

While the arguments and analyses presented in *Queering the Museum* unfold as the book progresses, each chapter can nevertheless be read as a free-standing engagement with a specific set of practices, issues, and challenges. If this is the approach the reader chooses to take, we recommend beginning with Chapter 1 since this sets out the museological context in which the notion of queering the museum emerged, the limitations of inclusion discourse to which it is a response, and the theoretical framework for the book as a whole.

Chapter 1 begins with the premise that museological practice is constructed, changing, and open to radical rethinking. Turning our attention to the dominant understanding of 'the museum' (whilst simultaneously acknowledging that there are differences within and between museums) we interrogate the epistemological underpinnings of museological practice and the ways in which these are informed by and contribute to heteronormative ways of knowing, doing, and being. Our analysis employs critical tools and insights developed by queer theorists, thereby allowing us to address questions of gender and sexuality and their relationship to the structural roots of exclusion in museums, whilst avoiding reproducing the assimilationist logic[20] oftentimes found in social inclusion discourse and its associated identity-based practices. At the same time, we suggest that the systemic privileging of heterosexuality and cisgender in museums (as elsewhere) is inextricable from the privileging of whiteness, able-bodiedness, and class privilege, and consequently we propose an intersectional approach to the critique of museological practice.

This chapter also offers an account of Pierre Bourdieu's (1990) notion of habitus in order to think through how embodied dispositions – naturalised ways of knowing and doing – are inculcated in and through practices of professionalisation, and to explain how museum conventions work through individuals at the level of sensibility – something 'feels' 'right' or 'wrong', 'professional' or 'amateurish'. In working through us, habitus constitutes us as particular kinds of individuals belonging to a specific (in this case, professional) community, and positions us relative to others in that community, or, as Bourdieu calls it, field. This is not to imply that habitus is wholly determined and/or determining, but it is to suggest that the idea that we can change our practice simply because we choose to is inadequate to the task of ethico-political intervention: we need to understand why change is much more difficult than we might like to assume. Bourdieu's account of how inherited ways of knowing, doing, and being are internalised, naturalised, and are thus difficult to both see and challenge, paves the way for a rethinking of ethics. In the museum sector, ethics is generally understood in terms of codes of practice consisting of principles and/or minimum standards that museum professionals are expected to be familiar with and guided by. This approach to, and understanding of, ethics presupposes that the individuals for whom such codes are written, are wholly self-transparent, rational, objective beings whose sense of who they are and what they do is separate from the professional context in which they operate. Drawing on poststructuralist accounts of ethics that queer these assumptions about identity (or subjectivity), and sociality, we introduce an understanding of ethics as critical practice, one that acknowledges the situated, embodied character of knowing, doing, and being, and at the same time, experiments with alternatives.

Chapter 2 focusses on the politics and practice(s) of display and begins by asking how we might respond to the absence (or at least the marginalisation) in museums of some histories, lives, identities, relations, issues, and practices, and the ubiquity of others. Rather than simply proposing a more inclusive approach to representation, whereby traditionally excluded groups, knowledges, ideas, and so on, are included, and diversity is envisaged as positive, this chapter interrogates what we might think of as the microtechnologies of curatorial practice – object choice, interpretation, labelling, placement, framing, duration of display – that shape representation and contribute to world-making. These practices, we argue, are performative (Butler, 1999): they are shaped by inherited codes and conventions that become naturalised through repetition, and they reproduce – albeit inadvertently – established and dominant ways of knowing, doing, and being and the privileges and exclusions they engender. Our approach in this chapter is to discuss examples of interventions that – from our perspective at least – at once critically engage with heteronormative conventions, practices, and the assumptions that support them, and articulate other ways of responding to absence; in short, examples of queer(ing) practice.

In Chapter 3 we explore the tension between the opening up of interpretation in museums and the continued hierarchisation of ways of knowing and being, between, we might say, inclusion and exclusion, diversity and uniformity. Our analysis of interpretation practices – most specifically labelling and cataloguing – and the epistemological assumptions that underpin them, problematises both the belief that meaning is inherent in objects, and the pluralist/inclusive approach to 'multiple ontologies'. Drawing on the work of Bruno Latour (1987, 2004, 2005), we suggest a move away from the question of what things *mean* and towards an analysis of what things *do*, how and why. We explore this shift via a focus on collections management practices and documentation which, we argue, are so naturalised and normalised within the museum sector that little work, academically and otherwise, has been done to critically interrogate them and the effects they produce. Drawing on the work of Geoffrey Swinney, we ask, "what do we know about what we 'know' about our collections?" (Swinney, 2012:35), and how might we know, and thus catalogue/document, differently?

One of the most fraught issues in contemporary museological practice and scholarship is community engagement, in particular, the question of how to enable a repositioning of visitors from "users and choosers to makers and shapers" (Cornwall & Gaventa, cited in Lynch, 2011:441) in order to trouble established relations of power and privilege. This imperative – whether it is enshrined in government policy, or driven by an increasingly widespread feeling that inclusion is morally correct – all too often tends to bring out the worst in museum professionals. Interestingly, an in-depth critical analysis of why this might be so is almost entirely absent in museological literature. Instead what one finds is a plethora of articles that detail how museums *should* engage with communities on equal terms, and a rather smaller number that use case studies to illuminate the shortcomings of attempts to do so. Chapter 4 tackles this by first queering the heteronormative notion of community and the assumptions that underpin it. Articulating an account of community that was always already heterogeneous and fractured (Secomb, 2000, 1997), we call for a rethinking of the productive potential of contestation (as opposed to the ideal of consensus). We then engage with three examples of collaborative projects that move away from a conception of community as what Latour refers to as a "matter of fact" and toward an understanding of community as a "matter of interest/concern". This latter approach, we argue, is able to acknowledge complexity and intersectionality and reimagine collaboration through the adoption of alternative epistemologies. Throughout our analyses we focus on processes as well as outcomes, and thus demonstrate the importance of paying close critical attention to the situatedness of collaborations and the institutional, social, political, and cultural factors that influence them. This shift in focus, which is apparent in all three examples discussed, enables a rethinking of value judgements that circumscribe the success, or otherwise, of community engagement, and articulates a queer/ing of collaboration as always already complex, networked, in process, and never complete.

Queering the Museum offers, as we said earlier, a range of flexible tools and insights that can be adopted, adapted, expanded, and critiqued by museum practitioners and scholars, and, as such, should by no means be regarded as the final word on queer museological practice. Indeed, the book is, undoubtedly, limited, partial, and imperfect, but from a queer perspective, this is as it should be.[21] Our hope is that *Queering the Museum* will foment thinking in this area, and create openings for ongoing critical interventions and futural imaginings.

Notes

1 This is also the case for other marginalised groups, and is reflected in composition of the museum workforce. For a report on the improvements and the ongoing failures in the arts and cultural sector in the UK with regard to fostering diverse workplaces, see the Arts Council of England's Equality, Diversity and

the Creative Case (2018). The situation in the UK is not significantly different from that of the USA, Australia, or Canada.

2 MONA's operational costs are underpinned by the winery, brewery, and restaurant on the same site. MONA also offers a $75,000 membership programme called "Eternity Membership", which includes lifetime free admission and allegedly earns members the right to be cremated and their remains housed in a "fancy Julia deVille-designed urn in the museum". See https://mona.net.au/stay/cinerarium.

3 MONA's display of inverted neon crosses around Hobart's waterfront during the 2018 Dark MOFO festival in 2018 attracted much criticism and prompted 1,500 people to sign a petition to have the crosses removed. The previous year Dark MOFO created headlines with Austrian artist Hermann Nitsch's three-hour installation, *150 Action*, which made use of fish and bull carcasses, milk, and animal blood. Animal Liberation Tasmania put together a petition which garnered around 12,500 signatures.

4 Veteran art collector John Kaldor suggests that the second tier of private museums that is slowly emerging in Australia, of which MONA is an example, "are not accountable to governments and boards, and they don't have to sell work, so they can be more adventurous. People don't have to agree with what is being shown, but it offers a different insight into the art world. This diversity is a sign of a coming of age in Australia". See www.theage.com.au/entertainment/art-and-design/the-collector-20070414-ge4ng8.html Accessed 20 November 2018.

5 See https://icom.museum/en/faq/what-is-icoms-definition-of-a-museum/ Accessed 15 April 2018.

6 See https://icom.museum/en/activities/standards-guidelines/museum-definition/ Accessed 01 March 2019.

7 In the landmark *Museums and the Shaping of Knowledge*, Hooper-Greenhill convincingly demonstrates that "it is a mistake to assume that there is only one form of reality for museums, only one fixed mode of operating. Looking back into the history of museums, the realities of museums have changed many times" (1992:1).

8 O'Neill cites Appleton (2002, 2001), de Montebello (2001), and Tusa (2000) as exemplifying this tendency. De Montebello was Director of New York's Metropolitan Museum of Art from 1997 to 2008.

9 These are all examples that Appleton gives.

10 Well-known and oft-cited advocates of this position include Sandell (2002, 2003, 2016), Janes and Sandell (2018), Sandell and Nightingale (2012), Fleming (2016, 2012, 2002), Dodd (2002), Gurian (2005), and Message (2014).

11 Like Bennet, we use the term 'technology' throughout this book, not in the narrow sense to refer to what we might think of as 'hard technologies' such as industrial machines, computers, smartphone apps, and so on. Rather, technology, as we understand it, has at its heart the Greek *tekhnē*, meaning to craft, make, fabricate, and the Greek *logy/logia*, meaning a speaking, discourse, theory. Thus technologies are the means by which we articulate the world both epistemologically and materially.

12 See also Bennett, who writes "Museums now seem self-evidently to be parts of more globalized flows of information, people, ideas". Even though they are "creations of national, municipal or local governments or private organizations, [they] reach out not only beyond their own walls but also beyond national boundaries through new practices of Web-curation" (2006:47).

13 Marxist theorist Antonio Gramsci introduced the notion of cultural hegemony to explain the ways in which a governing power (for example the ruling class) wins consent to its rule from those it subjugates. Hegemonic power is antithetical to, and far less visible and open to contestation than, authoritarian rule, since it appears natural and inevitable.
14 See, for example, AAM (2010); The Audience Agency (2018).
15 We are mindful of the fact that some academics do undertake work in museums. However, for the most part they do this as 'outsiders' whose roles, opportunities, constraints, and concerns are significantly different to 'internal' museum staff. This issue is explored in more detail in relation to artists and guest curators in Chapter 2.
16 The Centre of Democracy opened in May 2017 as a collaboration led by the History Trust of South Australia with the State Library of South Australia. Prior to this there had been no museum dedicated to the political history of the state since at least 1995, when the Constitutional Museum at Old Parliament House, formally managed by the History Trust of South Australia, closed.
17 There are currently a number of edited collections whose aim is to bring museological theory and practice together around notions of gender and sexuality. See, for example, Levin (2010) and Janes and Sandell (2018). There are also a number of rich, informative, and inspiring books that engage with museum practice and its capacity to challenge heteronormativity whose authors are academics that are involved in museological practice. For example, see Sandell (2017), Tyburczy (2016), and Geismar (2018).
18 In some cases, we have undertaken extensive discussions with colleagues in other institutions.
19 Many of the interventions we analyse have associated PhD theses and/or publications that critically engage with the processes underpinning their development, or aspects thereof.
20 The aim of assimilationist groups was (and still is) to be accepted into, and to become one with, mainstream culture. Consequently, one of the primary tenets of assimilationist discourses is the belief in a common humanity to which both homosexuals and heterosexuals belong. And this commonality – the fact that we are all human beings despite differences in secondary characteristics such as the gender of our sexual object choices – is the basis, it is claimed, on which we should all be accorded the same (human) rights, and on which we should treat each other with tolerance and respect. For an account of the role of assimilationism in LGBT politics and activism historically, see Sullivan (2003).
21 There is much the book does not engage with, for example, the role and practice of education departments and programmes in museums, visitor behaviour and studies, human resources, and governance. However, it is our hope that the analyses we offer will nevertheless have relevance to those working in areas of the sector that both the brevity of the book, and our own lack of experience, has prohibited us from discussing.

References

American Association of Museums. (2010). *Demographic Transformation and the Future of Museums*. Washington: The AAM Press.

Appleton, J. (2002). Distorted Priorities Are Destroying Local Museums. *The Independent*, May 29. www.independent.co.uk/voices/commentators/josie-appleton-distorted-priorities-are-destroying-local-museums-190408.html

Appleton, J. (2001). *Museums for 'The People'?* London: Academy of Ideas.

Arts Council England. (2018). *Equality, Diversity and the Creative Case: A Data Report, 2017–2018*. www.artscouncil.org.uk/publication/equality-diversity-and-creative-case-data-report-2016-17

The Audience Agency. (2018). *Museums Audience Report*. London. www.theaudienceagency.org/asset/1707

Bennett, T. (2006). Exhibition, Difference, and the Logic of Culture. In I. Karp, C. A. Kratz, L. Szwaja, & T. Ybarra-Frausto (Eds.), *Museum Frictions: Public Cultures/Global Transformations* (pp. 46–69). Durham: Duke University Press.

Bennett, T. (2005). Civic Laboratories: Museums, Cultural Objecthood and the Governance of the Social. *Cultural Studies*, 19(5), 521–547.

Bennett, T. (1995). *The Birth of the Museum*. London: Routledge.

Bourdieu, P. (1990). *The Logic of Practice*. Stanford, CA: Stanford University Press.

Butler, J. (1999). Bodies That Matter. In J. Price & M. Shildrick (Eds.), *Feminist Theory and the Body: A Reader* (pp. 235–245). Edinburgh: Edinburgh University Press.

Conlan, A. (2010). Representing Possibility: Morning, Memorial, and Queer Museology. In A. K. Levin (Ed.), *Gender, Sexuality and Museums: A Routledge Reader* (pp. 253–263). London and New York: Routledge.

de Montebello, P. (2001). The Art Museum's Most Valuable Currency: Curatorial Expertise. *The Art Newspaper*, 12(111), 10.

Dewdney, A., Dibosa, D., & Walsh, V. (2012). Cultural Diversity: Politics, Policy and Practices. The case of Tate Encounters. In R. Sandell & E. Nightingale (Eds.), *Museums, Equality and Social Justice* (pp. 114–24). London & New York: Routledge.

Dewdney, A., Dibosa, D., & Walsh, V. (2013). *Post Critical Museology: Theory and Practice in the Art Museum*. London: Routledge.

Diprose, R. (1994). *The Bodies of Women: Ethics, Embodiment, and Sexual Difference*. London: Routledge.

Dodd, J. (2002). Museums and the Health of the Community. In R. Sandell (Ed.), *Museums, Society, Inequality* (pp. 213–224). London: Routledge.

Fleming, D. (2016). Do Museums Change Lives? Ninth Stephen Weil Memorial Lecture. *Curator: The Museum Journal*, 59(2), 73–79.

Fleming, D. (2012). Museums for Social Justice: Managing Organisational Change. In R. Sandell & E. Nightingale (Eds.), *Museums, Equality and Social Justice* (pp. 72–83). London: Routledge.

Fleming, D. (2002). Positioning the Museum for Social Inclusion. In R. Sandell (Ed.), *Museums, Society, Inequality* (pp. 213–224). London: Routledge.

Geismar, H. (2018). *Museum Object Lessons for the Digital Age*. London: UCL Press.

Gurian, E. H. (2005). *Civilizing the Museum: The Selected Writings of Elaine Heumann Gurian*. London: Routledge.

Heimlich, J., & Koke, J. (2008). Gay and Lesbian Visitors and Cultural Institutions: Do They Come? Do They Care? A Pilot Study. *Museums & Social Issues: A Journal of Reflective Discourse*, 3(1), 93–104.

Hooper-Greenhill, E. (2000). Museums and the Interpretation of Visual Culture. London: Routledge.

Hooper-Greenhill, E. (1992). *Museums and the Shaping of Knowledge*. London: Routledge.

Janes, R. R., & Sandell, R. (2018). *Museum Activism*. London: Routledge.

Latour, B. (2005). From Realpolitik to Dingpolitik, or How to Make Things Public. In B. Latour & P. Weibel (Eds.), *Making Things Public: Atmospheres of Democracy* (pp. 14–43). Cambridge, MA: Mit Press.

Latour, B. (2004). Why Has Critique Run Out of Steam? From Matters of Fact to Matters of Concern. *Critical Inquiry*, 30(2), 225–248.

Latour, B. (1987). *Science in Action: How to Follow Scientists and Engineers Through Society*. Cambridge, MA: Harvard University Press.

Levin, A. (2012). *Museums, Equality and Social Justice*. London and New York: Routledge.

Levin, A. (Ed.) (2010). *Gender, Sexuality & Museums*. London & New York: Routledge.

Lewis, G. D. (2019). Types of Museums. *Encyclopaedia Brittanica*. www.britannica.com/topic/museum-cultural-institution/Types-of-museums

Lynch, B. (2011). Custom-Made Reflective Practice: Can Museums Realise Their Capabilities in Helping Others Realise Theirs? *Museum Management and Curatorship*, 26(5), 441–458.

McIntyre, D. (2007). What to Collect? Museums and Lesbian, Gay, Bisexual, and Transgender Collecting. *International Journal of Art and Design Education*, 26(1), 48–53.

Message, K. (2014). *Museums and Social Activism: Engaged Protest*. London: Routledge.

Mulhearn, D. (2015). Untold Stories. *Museums Journal*, 115(9), 20–25.

Museums Association. (2017). *Museums Change Lives*. www.museumsassociation.org/download?id=1218885

O'Neill, M. (2006). Essentialism, Adaptation and Justice: Towards a New Epistemology of Museums. *Museum Management and Curatorship*, 21(2), 95–116.

Pearce, E. (2015). More Mona. *MONA Blog*, September 17, https://mona.net.au/blog/2015/09/more-mona

Sandell, R. (2017). *Museums, Moralities, and Human Rights*. London: Routledge.

Sandell, R. (2003). Social Inclusion, the Museum, and the Dynamics of Sectoral Change. *Museum and Society*, 1(1), 45–62.

Sandell, R. (2002). *Museums, Society, Inequality*. London: Routledge.

Sandell, R., & E. Nightingale. (2012). *Museums, Equality and Social Justice*. London: Routledge.

Secomb, L. (2000). Fractured Community. *Hypatia*, 15(2), 133–150.

Secomb, L. (1997). Queering Community. In *Queerzone*. Nepean: University of Western Sydney Women's Research Centre.

Sherman, D., & Rogoff, I. (1994). *Museum Culture: Histories, Discourses, Spectacles*. Minneapolis: University of Minnesota Press.

Sullivan, N. (2003). *A Critical Introduction to Queer Theory*. Edinburgh: Edinburgh University Press.

Swinney, G. (2012). What Do We Know About What We Know? The Museum "register" as Museum Object. In S. Dudley, A. J. Barners, J. Binnie, J. Petrou, & J. Walklate (Eds.), *The Thing About Museums: Objects and Experience, Representation and Contestation* (pp. 31–46). London and New York: Routledge.

Tusa, J. (2000). *Art Matters: Reflecting on Culture*. London: Methuen.

Tyburczy, J. (2016). *Sex Museums: The Politics and Performance of Display*. Chicago: University of Chicago Press.

Vanegas, A. (2010). Representing Lesbians and Gay Men in British Social History Museums. In A. K. Levin (Ed.), *Gender, Sexuality and Museums: A Routledge Reader* (pp. 163–171). London and New York: Routledge.

Weil, S. (1994). The Proper Business of the Museum: Ideas or Things? In G. Kavanagh (Ed.), *Museum Provision and Professionalism* (pp. 79–86). London: Routledge.

1 From LGBTIQ+ inclusion to queer ethics

As Helen Rees Leahy (2012) and Tony Bennett (1995) have demonstrated, from their inception, museums have cultivated suitable publics through the use of changing strategies and techniques. At the same time, they have, both intentionally and inadvertently, excluded those whose being-in-the-world does not fit with the normative structures and rationalities[1] of such institutions. One example of this is the absence in museums internationally of lesbian, gay, bisexual, transgender, intersex, and queer (LGBTIQ+) lives, experiences, and histories. Research suggests that this sort of exclusion negatively impacts LGBTIQ+ people, their families, and allies in a variety of ways. As Charles Taylor explains,

> a person or group of people can suffer real damage, real distortion, if the people or society around them mirror back to them a confining or demeaning or contemptible picture of themselves. . . . Nonrecognition or misrecognition can inflict harm, can be a form of oppression, imprisoning someone in a . . . reduced mode of being.
>
> (1994:25)

Similarly, Anna Conlan argues that, "omission from the museum does not simply mean marginalization; it formally classifies certain lives, histories, and practices as insignificant, renders them invisible, marks them as unintelligible, and thereby casts them into the realm of the unreal" (2010:257). According to Judith Butler, this construction of excluded others is inseparable from the construction of the norm, the subject, the centre: indeed, the former provides the contrast against which the subject, the norm, defines itself, and accrues its status (1993/2011:xiii).

In recent years there has been a growing perception in the Galleries, Libraries, Archives, and Museums (GLAM) sector that cultural institutions have an obligation to reflect diversity in all its forms, to take an active approach to inclusion, equality, and social justice, and to promote understanding between different groups, communities, and cultures (Nightingale & Sandell, 2013). To date, concerns such as these have been articulated primarily in terms of social exclusion/inclusion, human rights, and civic or moral responsibility (Sandell, 2017). While interventions undertaken in this conceptual vein are commendable, we contend that, in practice, inclusion strategies often fail to really grapple with the complexities of difference, of lived, embodied histories and habituated dispositions, or to undertake the kind of critical self-reflection that is imperative if museums are to play an active role in radical change.

Social inclusion

Critiques of exclusion and political demands for recognition in and by cultural institutions are far from new. For decades feminists, artists of colour, and others have identified, criticised, and attempted to counter the massive over-representation of white, upper-class, able-bodied, cisgender men in positions of power in cultural institutions, and the works, perspectives, objects, and histories of such men in art galleries and museums (Nochlin, 1971; White, 1976; Piper, 1996; Mũnoz, 1999). Cultural practitioners such as Deborah Willis, Coco Fusco, Lisa Reihana, Mat Fraser, and the Unbound Collective, to mention just a few, have also highlighted and critiqued the fact that when marginalised groups have been included it has largely been as subaltern[2] others, as objects rather than subjects of art, history, science, anthropology, and so on. While critical interventions that focus on difference and the structures of differentiation that (re)produce hierarchical relations and inequalities are almost always politically radical, the same cannot, we contend, be said of social inclusion discourse, rooted, as it is, in governmental policy.

Social inclusion, as a governmental discourse that interpolates cultural institutions, emerged in the UK in the 1990s under New Labour. Through a number of social inclusion policy moves (DCMS, 1999, 2000a, 2000b, 2005) museums, galleries, and archives were called upon to attract new publics and tackle social exclusion by linking their services to the four main indicators of social exclusion identified by the government: poor health, high crime, low educational attainment, and unemployment (Kinsley, 2016:476; Sandell, 2003:46). As Chris Smith, the then UK Secretary of State, put it in 2000, "museums, galleries and archives can act as agents of social change in the community, improving the quality of people's lives through their outreach activities" (DCMS, 2000a:3). Consequently, museums and other cultural institutions began developing policies and practices aimed at enabling people to develop confidence, resilience, and a sense of belonging; expand their knowledge, skills, and qualifications; increase their employability; and improve overall wellbeing. While on the face of it this may sound laudable, the imperative that drove social inclusion policy was to "improve human capacity and 'capital'" (Message, 2013:209) and minimise dependence on the state.

The motivations of museum staff involved in the development and implementation of inclusion strategies are undoubtedly many and varied, but anecdotal evidence suggests that, on the whole, they do not simply conform to the neoliberal agenda articulated by New Labour. Indeed, social inclusion discourse and policy has been leveraged to justify and fund programmes, events, and strategies that might be viewed in mainstream terms as 'overtly political', or at least 'contentious'. In our own museums we have used the South Australian Department of Communities and Social Inclusion's LGBTIQ Inclusion Strategy (DCSI, 2014) as the basis for a queer action plan, and as a rejoinder to a small number of visitor complaints about *OUT at the Museum*, an exhibition by and about queer youth which we discuss in Chapter 4. While, as Kylie Message notes, "Australian governments have not developed equivalent policy frameworks linking social outcomes to cultural policy and giving museums a clear purposeful directive" (Message, 2013:208), in the last few years social inclusion strategies and guidelines for developing inclusive workplaces and practices have been produced by a number of state governments (DPC, 2016; PSC, 2017; CSRDPC, 2015), and sectoral interventions are often framed in these terms.

Despite the fact that the notion of social inclusion can and has been used as a tool with which to begin to highlight the biases associated with traditional museological idea(l)s and practices, it is nevertheless our contention that social inclusion discourse aims to align individuals with the heteronormative aims of the state. In doing so, it functions as what Dewdney, Dibosa, and Walsh refer to as a "containment strategy" that ensures "that demands for change are neutralised" (2012:115). The tension between a radical politics of difference and inclusion policies and practices plays out in complex and often contradictory ways in museums. At worst, it manifests as a form of "cultural instrumentalism" which in its drive to achieve "greater market reach at the margins of the market" (Dewdney et al., 2012:117), invariably reduces marginalised 'others' to commodities that institutions can utilise to "acquire or maintain a competitive edge in the market" (Iverson, 2007:600). Further, statements of commitment to inclusion and diversity (such as those that appear on museum websites) can function as a disavowal of the fact that an institution may – at least in some aspects of its operation – be exclusionary, racist, homophobic, ableist, and so on, and thus inhibit the critical self-reflection that is integral to a genuine commitment to change.[3]

Dewdney et al.'s analysis of social inclusion policy and its implementation in the museum sector in the UK supports these criticisms, demonstrating that the imposition of diversity indicators tied to funding means, for example, that 'blackness' "functions less as a political position from which to critique power, than as a skin-colour, and an identifiable, quantifiable indicator of a particular group" (2012:116). The same could be said about gender, disability, and sexuality. 'Auditable diversity', as Dewdney et al. refer to it, thus constructs the difference it presumes to be visibly self-evident, *as* self-evident, as innate, fixed, essential: it reaffirms the essentialist notion of identity as inherent and fixed and thereby fails to interrogate the ways in which "museums serve as disciplinary structures, socially constructed means of defining and regulating difference" (Wallis, 2003:179).[4] For Dewdney et al., this sort of approach constitutes what they, following Kobena Mercer, describe as "a detachment from the radicalism of 'difference' in order to attain the de-radicalised aims of diversity" (2012:116). Nathan Sentance makes a similar critique arguing that while "Many libraries, archives and museums . . . talk about how they value diversity and many . . . have their own diversity and inclusion initiatives. . . . These are often shallow exercises. . . [that] are seldom created to challenge and disrupt whiteness within and outside the sector" (2018:npn). Drawing on Poka Laenui's discussion of the fifth step of colonisation – in which aspects of traditional culture that refuse to die are appropriated and assimilated into the culture of the dominating colonial society (2006:2)[5] – Sentenace suggests that inclusion and diversity initiatives can, and do, appropriate (and thus further exploit) colonised others in their construction of mainstream culture as liberal, enlightened, egalitarian, and so on. Muñoz-Reed supports this, arguing that "Systematically including oppressed histories into the museum has proven to be insufficient, and in fact, when not carefully enacted, has led to an institutional tokenism, which has only served to reinforce imperial power hierarchies" (2017:101).

It is undoubtedly easier for museums to take a "pragmatic approach" to calls for inclusion by adding on services that do not challenge the structure of the museum and the principles that underpin it (O'Neill, 2002:36) than to address the structural roots of exclusion. Our own practice as curators (or, as we'd like to think, curatorial activists) has convinced us of the veracity of Richard Sandell's claim that a paradigm shift is essential (2003:45) if we are to reconfigure museums as sites of radical contestation and debate. For us, this entails moving beyond (when and where appropriate) inclusion, to a 'queering' of contemporary museum practices, the often-invisible assumptions that underpin them, and the effects they produce.

Such an approach entails, first, acknowledging that there has been little attention paid by museum professionals to the ways in which museological theory and practice have constructed sexual norms, or to the role each of us, as practitioners, plays in the maintenance of heteronormativity (Saunders,

2008:15–16). Heteronormativity, as Lauren Berlant and Michael Warner define it, refers to

> the institutions, structures of understanding, and practical orientations that make heterosexuality seem not only coherent – that is, organized as a sexuality – but also privileged. Its coherence is always provisional, and its privilege can take several (sometimes contradictory) forms: unmarked as the idiom of the personal and the social; or marked as a natural state; or projected as an ideal or moral accomplishment. It consists less of norms that could be summarized as a body of doctrine than as a sense of rightness produced in contradictory manifestations – often unconscious, immanent to practice or to institutions.
>
> (1998:548)

This term has been used in a variety of ways with some authors focussing solely on sexuality and others on gender and sexuality.[6] We want to suggest that insofar as identity and positionality are always effects of complex intersecting vectors of power and privilege a single focus on sexuality and/or gender is problematic. Drawing on scholarship on intersectionality (Crenshaw, 1991) we propose that critiques of heteronormativity must pay critical attention to the ways in which the systemic privileging of heterosexuality and cisgender[7] is inextricable from the privileging of whiteness, able-bodiedness, class privilege, and so on. As Barnard puts it, "race and sexuality are not two separate axes of identity that cross and overlay in particular subject positions, but rather, ways to circumscribe systems of meaning and understanding that formatively and inherently define each other" (1999:200). Similarly, Mollow and McRuer gesture towards the inextricability of sex and dis/able-bodiedness in their assertion that "able-bodiedness is the foundation of sexiness. . . . Rarely are disabled people regarded as either desiring subjects or objects of desire" (2012:1).

In envisaging the critique of heteronormativity as intersectional we are not suggesting that, for example, racism and homophobia are 'the same', nor do we mean to conflate different forms of systemic violence, or to reduce complex, heterogeneous forms of marginalisation to a single term and thereby give precedence to sexuality over race, class, and so on. Rather, we contend that interrogating the othering of 'non-normative' knowledges and identities *together* can contribute to a mutually informing troubling of ableist, classist, colonialist, and heteronormative discourses, the assumptions that underpin and are reaffirmed by them, and the material effects they produce. On a more practical note, an intersectional approach to museological practice not only moves beyond the problematics of social inclusion that we outlined earlier, it also bypasses what some museum professionals might see as "the daunting task of fitting an ever-expanding rainbow of identities into existing museum archives, programs and exhibits" (Robert, 2014:25).

Critical analyses of the role of visual and/or material cultures in the (re)production of norms around identity and difference are, as we said earlier, far from new and yet they seem to have had little impact on museological practice. Indeed, as Tyburczy notes, there is a widespread failure to recognise that all museums have "always participated in the disciplining of sexuality" (Tyburczy, 2016:1), just as they have in the disciplining of gender, race, ethnicity, dis/ability, class, and so on. Why might this be?

Embodied knowledge

In order to begin to respond to this question it is necessary to consider the ways in which particular knowledges, practices, and identities become so normalised that their transmission or reproduction most often goes unnoticed and unremarked upon. The work of sociologist Pierre Bourdieu is helpful in unpacking the everyday processes that shape who are, what and how we know, how we act, our position in a particular context, and the relations between these things. In providing tools for critical analysis Bourdieu's work also opens up possibilities for other ways of being.

As Bourdieu understands it, we inherit and internalise ways of knowing, doing, and being through processes of socialisation. Professionalisation is one such process: we become professionals (curators, physiotherapists, footballers) through the internalisation or embodiment of inherited forms of knowledge and practice that become increasingly naturalised and therefore difficult to 'see' or to throw off. This is because "they make me who I am" (Haraway, 2004a:1):[8] knowing what particular objects mean, what their histories are likely to be, and how they should be handled makes me a curator, just as knowing how to read the pitch, outwit the person marking you, and drive a ball into a very small space at exactly the right moment, makes you a (good) footballer. The more this knowledge becomes 'second nature' the more professional one appears to others, and the more one identifies (and is identified) as a curator, a footballer, a physiotherapist.

The reproduction of inherited ways of knowing, doing, and being is not necessarily intentional nor is it wholly conscious; rather, it is an effect of what Bourdieu (1980) calls 'habitus'. Bourdieu uses this term to refer to the embodied dispositions that each of us acquires through processes of socialisation. These dispositions shape the ways in which we perceive and operate in the various contexts in which we find ourselves. Habitus is "the way society becomes deposited in persons in the form of lasting dispositions, or trained capacities and structured propensities to think, feel and act in determinant ways, which then guide them" (Wacquant, 2005:316).

Our gut feelings, attitudes, mannerisms, tastes, moral schemas, likes and dislikes, hopes and fears, orientations, are all an effect of habitus, as is our comportment, the language we use, the way we speak, physically interact with others, and relate to objects. These dispositions are generally shared by those with similar backgrounds (in particular in terms of class, ethnicity, education, and so on) and/or by those who belong to a shared organisational culture (such as a museum). They are so deeply ingrained in who we are that they feel natural, uncontestable, and, consequently, we pay them little critical attention: as Bourdieu explains, to be committed to and invested in a shared organisational culture (or field), what we have learned must take on the mantle of the obvious, its constructedness must be forgotten (1998:76–77).

Michel Foucault provides a wonderful illustration of this when, in a discussion of systems of classification and the ways in which they shape the world we inhabit, what and how we know, and our sense of ourselves and others, he cites a taxonomy allegedly found in an ancient Chinese encyclopaedia. Before we share it here, we want to reflect for a moment on the systems of classification that structure contemporary museological practice and that are taken for granted, assumed to be self-evident and rational. For most of us who work in museums, the idea that textiles are categorically different to ceramics and to mineral, or biological science specimens is a 'no brainer', indeed many of our museums are founded on such logic: as a social history museum, the Migration Museum (at which one of us works) does not collect sculptures or human or animal remains.[9] The same could be said of the classification of works in an art museum as sculpture, painting, ceramic, decorative, and so on. In assuming that these taxonomies reflect natural divisions, or simply taking them at face value – rather than seeing them as cultural fictions that far from simply describing the world, shape it – we reproduce inherited ways of knowing, doing, and being, and exclude others. Just imagine for a moment that a natural history museum decided to abandon the classification of animals into vertebrates and invertebrates, and into the many subgroups that come under them, and instead to classify them according to the following taxonomy that Foucault cites.

> Animals are divided into: (a) belonging to the Emperor, (b) embalmed, (c) tame, (d) sucking pigs, (e) sirens, (f) fabulous, (g) stray dogs, (h) included in the present classification, (i) frenzied, (j) innumerable, (k) drawn with a very fine camel-hair brush, (l) et cetera, (m) having just broken the water pitcher, (n) that from a long way off look like flies.
>
> (Foucault, 2005:xvi)

We imagine that both the museum practitioners who were asked to use this taxonomy as the basis of their practice, and the visitors to the museum, would be at best confused, and at worst seriously troubled by what appears to be the nonsensicality of a such a system. Such responses would, we suggest, be deeply felt, rather than just intellectual: curators tasked to employ this system would probably feel anxious, as if what they were doing was wrong, and visitors may well lose faith in the museum and the authority they had previously accorded it, and literally turn away. This clearly illustrates "the limitation of our own [thought], the stark impossibility of thinking *that*" (Foucault, 2005:xvi), At the same time, it supports Bourdieu's claim that inherited ways of knowing, doing, and being are embodied and, over time, become 'second nature'. Consequently, through our everyday actions we reproduce, and further entrench, normalised epistemologies without, for the most part, realising that we do so.

Bourdieu refers to the embodiment and reproduction of norms as having a 'feel for the game', as an unconscious (or less-than-conscious), tacit, 'know-how', that makes us effective players ('professionals') within a particular field. As Bourdieu explains, "Having a feel for the game is having the game under the skin" (1998:80); a good player (a professional), he writes, "has the immanent tendencies of the game in her body, in an incorporated state: she embodies the game" (1998:81). This account runs counter to and challenges utilitarian theories of action which claim that the social behaviour of individuals is rational, intentional, conscious, and ends-driven.

For Bourdieu the social world is composed of fields, each with its own rules, rationales, practices, positions, and power relations, and its own underlying organising principles. Within these fields, individuals manoeuver in pursuit of desirable resources: these might range from the sense of a job well done, to a reputation for excellence, or the position of CEO. Bourdieu refers to these resources as capital, and explains that capital takes a number of (often, but not always, connected) forms: economic capital consists of money, assets, property; social capital is the name given to the networks and relationships of influence that grease the wheels of success; and cultural capital consists of the assets that promote social mobility, for example, education, styles of speech and dress, taste, particular cultural competencies, and so on. The more effectively one operates in a given field, the more capital one will accrue, and the more capital one has, the more likely one is to attain 'success' (however that is defined within the field). Moreover, the more capital one has the more one is able to influence the field and its operations, to determine what counts as 'good practice', as 'success', as capital. These value judgments that shape (and are shaped by) the field and the ways in which players operate within it, serve the interests of those who make them, ensuring their insider status, and their exclusivity.[10] At the same time, they exclude individuals, knowledges, and practices that do not or cannot 'fit', and this exclusion appears inevitable. For example, a person who does not have the necessary qualifications (such as a degree in Art History) or the required cultural competencies (such as a knowledge of and appreciation for contemporary art) is unlikely to be even considered for a curatorial position in a contemporary art museum.[11]

Drawing on the concepts we've outlined in this section, we suggest that it is useful to think of the museum sector as a field of practice, the core business (or key organising principle) of which has traditionally been understood to be the acquisition, conservation, and interpretation of objects deemed significant, and the provision of public access to these objects and the insights they embody. These practices have often been assumed to be largely apolitical and determined by empirical givens such as 'historical accuracy', 'significance', 'scientific facts', 'aesthetic quality', and so on. But as many before us have noted, decisions about what is (and what is not) collected and why, and how objects are classified, interpreted, displayed, and so on, are highly politicised, and full of bias (Parker & Pollock, 1981; Fleming, 2016; Watson, 2009; Steorn, 2012). This is also true – as we have seen – of the question of who makes such decisions, the criteria on which they are made, and the field in which such constructions are engendered as self-evident, inevitable, and uncontestable.

The fact that, like many museums, the museums that operate under the auspices of the History Trust of South Australia have a paucity of objects relating to LGBTIQ+ his/stories is not an historical accident, but nor, we suggest, is it simply the result of conscious and intentional bias on the behalf of curators past and present. Rather, in as much as museum practitioners "operate within the cultural space carved out by their predecessors" (Alberti, cited in Swinney, 2012:33), they tend to reproduce the habitus they inherit. This is not to suggest that change does not occur or, that when it does, it is not initiated by museum practitioners: for Bourdieu, habitus is neither wholly determined nor a result of free will, but rather, is always "a kind of interplay between the two over time" (Bourdieu, 1984:170). However, such change often tends to be superficial rather than substantive and this is because, as Bourdieu's account of habitus explains, the development of dispositions and competencies associated with a particular occupational culture is reliant on the embodiment, and tacit acceptance, of the underlying organising principles or rationales of that field. Consequently, radically different ways of knowing and doing are unlikely to occur to us, or, if they do, to feel 'wrong', 'unprofessional', or too risky.

For Bourdieu, structural organisational change is only possible if we can "undo the mechanisms of dehistoricisation and universalisation – 'always and everywhere has it been this way' – whereby arbitrary workings of power are enabled to continue" (Emirbayer & Johnson, 2008:47–48). His account of the way in which the principles of a particular field – in this case, the museum – "become deposited in persons in the form of lasting dispositions, or trained capacities and structured propensities to think, feel and act in determinant ways, which then guide them" (Wacquant, 2005:316) helps to explain why it appears to be easier for 'outsiders' to critically engage with a field of practice than it is for 'insiders' – an issue we will discuss in more detail in the following chapter. But it also explains why co-curation projects involving museum staff and 'outsiders' are almost always difficult for all involved. We will explore this tendency later in the book, but for now we want to consider the ways in which habituated idea(l)s about gender and sexuality have played out in museums.

LGBTIQ+ inclusion in museums

While the past decade or so may have ushered in significant changes in social norms around sexuality and gender it nevertheless remains the case that displays of heterosexuality and cisgender are ubiquitous in museums and as such function as the norm, the invisible centre against which otherness is defined (or, more correctly, constructed). Think for a moment of natural history museums, and of the displays of animals one often encounters there. Typical natural history tableaus feature animals and settings we associate with 'nature'. The former are often in groups (usually consisting of a male and a female, and sometimes offspring) that construct heterosexuality, the nuclear family, and normative gender roles as universal and natural (Levin, 2012:158). Such displays appear to offer a sense of unmediated vision of the 'natural' world; an objective, apolitical window onto a 'reality', an undeniable 'truth' that is simply there. But as Donna Haraway argues, 'realism' is the painfully constructed effect of technologies of mastery and meaning-making, that reduce the things displayed to objects (2004b:166). And nowhere is this more apparent than in taxidermic displays that necessitate the literal sacrifice of an other's life.

As the heated debates that broke out in the UK in 2017 around *Prejudice and Pride: Exploring LGBT History* illustrated all too painfully, in historic houses and heritage sites, as in museums, heterosexuality is presumed and thus (re)produced.[12] This assumption – often unapparent to those who make it until it is challenged – is reinforced through the (intentional and inadvertent) decisions made by curators and other professional staff to omit 'queerness'.[13] As Matt Smith and Richard Sandell explain, the stories told at historic houses are often based on family trees that map lineage and patterns of inheritance. As such, they tend to (re)produce heteronormative ways of knowing and being by erasing intimate relationships that did not result in marriage and/or offspring, and constructing those who did not marry simply as bachelors or spinsters. A generous interpretation might put this down to the fact that because, historically, same-sex relations and 'queer' gender expressions were at best stigmatised, and, at worst, illegal, and consequently were not well documented, those working in historic houses may be unaware of them. Or, if they are, they may feel that an absence of irrefutable proof of same-sex activity or gender queerness which, as Sandell notes, "would never be expected to prove someone's heterosexuality" (2017:75) or cisgender, would compromise 'historical accuracy' and thus undermine professional practice and identity. Such absences might also be indicative of dispositions that affect disinterest in or discomfort with 'queerness', or a fear of alienating visitors and/or entangling one's organisation in the kinds of scandals that erupted around exhibitions such as the Mapplethorpe retrospective *The Perfect Moment* (Corcoran Museum, 1989), *Hide/Seek: Difference and Desire in American Portraiture* (National Portrait Gallery, 2010), and *QUEERMUSEU* (Santander Cultural Center, 2017).

In short, then, the flip side of the pervasiveness of heterosexuality and cisgender in museums is that, historically, 'queer' identities, relations, and practices have rarely featured in museums, historic houses, and heritage sites. This is changing somewhat, and the last decade or so has seen an increase in the display of LGBTQ lives in museums (Frost, 2015:16).[14] However, inclusion in the space of the museum has, we contend, all too often meant inclusion in the parameters of sexual normalcy. Many of the temporary LGBTQ exhibitions that have taken place in the UK, USA, Australia, and some parts of Europe over the last decade or so have been characterised by a focus on identity-based histories, rights, and political struggles, and structured by a progressivist "grand narrative"[15] culminating, most recently, in marriage equality. Robert Mills cites the Museum of London's *Queer is Here* as one example of this, noting that a chronology of events deemed significant in the struggle for LGBT rights constituted over half of the exhibition (2010:81). This framing of lives that have been excluded from mainstream institutions in a progressivist narrative is undoubtedly important, but at the same time it tends to rely on and reproduce a number of problematic, deeply held assumptions and norms and, as Mills notes, to overlook queer lives and experiences that are not easily incorporated into an epistemology of the closet (2008:82).[16]

One such problem is that the temporal chronology that underpins progressivist narratives naturalises a notion of time that is particular to Western modernity and may have little or no relevance to those whose lives are structured around other ways of knowing and being. This kind of temporality is also linked to the concept of civilisation which situates non-Western cultures in the timeless past, and thus reproduces – most often unwittingly – "specific and exclusionary cultural values" (Robert, 2014:27).[17] Brigid Bosold and Vera Hofmann are likewise critical of what they see as the perpetuation of norms and exclusions in art exhibitions such as the Tate Britain's *Queer British Art 1861–1967* and The National Portrait Gallery's *Hide/Seek: Difference and Desire in American Portraiture*. Both, they write, reflect "prevailing social norms within the 'malestream' world" (2018:7) by over-representing (mostly white, cisgender, able-bodied) gay men and making "dykes, lesbian feminists, and queer women* 'invisible'" (2018:7). Brian Curtain adds the criticism that *Queer British Art 1861–1967* "arguably avows a homonationali[st] neoliberal co-optation of . . . homosexuality" (2018:14).

Perhaps chief amongst the normalising ideas that structure contemporary exhibitions of and engagements with LGBTIQ+ his/stories and issues is the conception of 'homosexuality' as an ahistorical, universal, and singular fact that has been "hidden from history" (Mills, 2008:48), rather than an umbrella term for a range of diverse, subject positions and practices that have been constructed, contested, lived, and experienced in multiple and complex ways. Consequently, the ways in which sex and/or gender identities are always already shaped by class, race, ethnicity, dis/ability, age, and so on, are rarely, if ever, given any real critical attention in exhibitions that foreground 'gay and lesbian history' (and assume it to be, amongst other things, singular, white, and able-bodied), an issue we will address at length in Chapter 2.

The essentialist understanding of 'homosexuality' and the associated idea that visibility, liberation, equality, and inclusion in the mainstream are the ultimate goals are, we argue, homonormative. Homonormativity, writes Lisa Duggan, is

> a politics that does not contest dominant heteronormative assumptions and institutions, but upholds and sustains them, while promising the possibility of a demobilized gay constituency and a privatized, depoliticized gay culture anchored in domesticity and consumption.
>
> (2004:50)

In other words, homonormativity plays into an assimilationist agenda – gays and lesbians get to take up the centre too – thereby sustaining, rather than contesting, heteronormativity. Same-sex marriage is, for some, a prime example of homonormativity. Tyburczy's (2014) critique of International Mr Leather – an international, though largely American, contest of leathermen held annually since 1979 – expands this to show that in some contexts homonormativity reaffirms normative body ideals (in this case cisgender and able-bodiedness) rather than institutions such as marriage. London's Natural History Museum's decision to open *Sexual Nature*, a temporary exhibition about sex in the so-called natural world, "just in time for Valentine's Day" (Millard, 2011), thereby reinforcing the association of sex with love, might also be read as homonormative. In their analysis of the exhibition Angela Cassidy, Simon J. Lock, and Georgina Voss argue that the representation of same-sex sexual behaviour in animals differentiated between 'innate' and 'circumstantial' homosexuality, casting the former as morally superior. Text panels characterised innate homosexuality as a "strong, often life-long attraction. . . [that] has a significant genetic and hormonal basis" (cited in Cassidy et al., 2016:224), whereas the display of adolescent male Adele penguins (as representative of circumstantial homosexuality) described their sex drives as "so strong, they will attempt to mate with anything". The use of the caption "Relax" on the text panel featuring the penguins, invoked, suggest Cassidy et al., "the 1983 song by Frankie Goes to Hollywood and its strong cultural connotation with clubbing, promiscuity and the AIDS era" (2016:224).[18]

What Cassidy et al.'s analysis highlights is the way in which homonormative displays simultaneously reaffirm heteronormative idea(l)s and construct (sometimes by implication rather than explicitly) those who won't or can't follow them as 'perverted'. So, while monogamous, middle-class, respectable, primarily white, cisgendered, able-bodied, gay and lesbian couples, and even monogamous same-sex animal couples, may be appearing in museums, polyamory, kink, gender queerness, communal living, sex work, intergenerational relations, queer bodies, lives, and relations remain conspicuous in their absence. While such absences may not explicitly prohibit queer sex, genders, and/or practices they nevertheless function as a "straightening device" (Ahmed, 2006:92), rendering queer sex, genders and practices as failures to follow the straight and narrow, as deviant, wrong, perverse and perverting. How then might museums engage with 'queerness' without producing reductive, normalising, de-radicalised, universalist stories? "How can radical queer, anti-assimilationist desire be translated into the museum without a tacit acknowledgment of the gaps, disruptions, geographical discrepancies and exceptions that such desires inflict upon the objective museum system?" (Winchester, 2012:143).

Queer/ing

Since the 1980s the term 'queer' – historically a derogatory term aimed at gay men – has been used as an umbrella term (a noun) by (some) people who identify as other than heterosexual and/or as gender diverse. At the same time, queer theorists have used the term to refer to a form of critical practice (that is, as a verb) that aims to trouble heteronormative knowledge, identities, and practices. This use of queer as a verb seems particularly apt given the term's etymology: queer is related to the German *quer*, meaning oblique, perverse, odd, and thus 'to queer' is to spoil, to put out of order, to make strange the taken-for-granted, the naturalised (Sullivan, 2003:52). As Isabel Hufschmidt puts it,

> *Queer* is not all rainbow colours and pink . . . but [rather, is about] how and why sexuality has served as a classificatory and policing tool in our culture. . . . [Q]ueer should not be understood merely as a credible practice for museums that are officially labelled 'gay' such as the Schwules Museum in Berlin. This is just the old practice of demarcation and segregation. . . . We have to go . . . farther and erase the . . . naturalized notion that *queer* is about 'minorities'; on the contrary, since it's about the construction of sexual categories . . . its clearly pan-social. *Queer* thinking thus, despite the misperceptions, trends away from the . . . niche towards the large macro-structures in our society.
>
> (2018:30)[19]

We might think of queer/ing, then, as a form of critical engagement that holds out "the promise of new meanings, new ways of thinking and acting politically" (Duggan, 1992:11).

Queering the museum, writes Amy Levin, requires "us to question every aspect of the institution" (2012:159). This entails critically interrogating not only the museological practices that are the lifeblood of museums, but also our own professional identities and dispositions. As we suggested earlier, like all professionals, museum practitioners are trained to ascribe meaning, evaluate, display, document, relate to and care for objects, and so on in accordance with the norms and conventions of a particular "occupational culture" (Liddiard, 2004:19). While such cultures vary – science museums, for example, may draw on and reproduce different idea(l)s and practices than social history museums or art galleries – they are all connected to and shaped by larger, inherited, socio-cultural systems that are particular to a given time and place. These large scale world-views or epistemologies, the shifts they have undergone, and their impact on museums, have been discussed in great detail by writers such as Elaine Hooper-Greenhill (1992), Tony Bennett (1995), and Sharon Macdonald (1998). While we do not have time to reiterate those analyses here, we'd like to note that within a given 'episteme'[20] there are always multiple world-views, and these different ways of knowing, doing, being are rarely accorded equal status. This becomes painfully apparent when, for example, the 'keepers' of collections are confronted with the world-views of source communities, in particular when issues such as repatriation are raised.

Rather than attempting to replace erroneous views of the past with true and correct ones, a queer approach is instead concerned with problematising heteronormative ways of knowing and the inequitable effects of such, and opening up possibilities for being, knowing, doing otherwise. Joshua Adair's (2017) work on historic house museums, in particular his reframing of the inability to conclusively define the gender and/or sexuality of an historical figure on the basis of uncontestable evidence as an opportunity for queer/ing practice rather than a reason to remain silent, is a good example of this. Adair reminds us that "we frequently catch glimpses of lives lived in ways that did not adhere to traditional narratives of gender and sexuality", and drawing on Elisa Giaccardi's notion of iridescence, argues for the need to "embrace the value of exploring possibility, of highlighting these moments when an object or subject iridesces" (2017:118). Giaccardi uses this term to refer to the way in which perception changes depending on perspective, on the position from which one sees: rather than assuming that past lives are monochromatic, a queer approach is alert to their multiplicity, to the ways in which they shimmer, diffract.[21]

What most interests us about this notion of iridescence is the radical challenge it poses to the subject of knowledge. As we said earlier, it has been widely assumed in museological practice that facts simply exist and can be accessed through rational observation, and that the role of the curator is to share these neutral 'truths' objectively. But feminist theorists have long challenged "the god trick of seeing everything from nowhere . . . the power to see and not be seen, to represent while escaping representation" (Haraway, 1988:581), arguing instead that knowledge is always situated and vision is always partial. In other words, what and how we see and know will depend on the habitus that shapes our perspective, on our position in the field, on the kind and amount of capital we have (or don't have), on our feel for the game: situated knowledges, writes Donna Haraway, "are about communities not about isolated individuals" (1988:590). This account of knowledge shifts debate away from the truth of a subject or object – for instance, the question of whether or not a historical figure 'really' was gay – and onto the construction of knowledge, the context in which it is produced, and the effects of such. Situated knowledge, Haraway writes "allows us to become answerable for what we learn to see" (1988:583) for the knowledge claims we make.[22] This is a particularly interesting claim in the context of museums given that interpretation is almost always framed as if from nowhere: curators rarely reveal themselves and their positionality, or suggest that the interpretation offered is, and can only ever be, partial and contingent. In Chapter 3 we consider how museum practitioners might queer the god trick of seeing everything from nowhere and acknowledge our positionality(s) and the roles we play in world-making.

The account of knowledge as always situated, partial, and perspectival that we have outlined here runs counter to and disrupts the all too common tendency to replace old mainstream truths with new historically marginalised ones. Far from making space for knowledge to iridesce, to be seen as multifaceted, complex, contradictory, and shifting, such an approach reproduces monochromatic logic and its exclusionary effects. Given this we take seriously Haraway's cautionary note that while those situated at the margins may be better placed to see the god trick, "the positionings of the subjugated are not exempt from critical reexamination. . . . The standpoints of the subjugated are not 'innocent' positions" (1988:584–585): they too are necessarily situated and partial. She writes,

> One cannot 'be' either a cell or a molecule or a woman, colonized person, laborer and so on, if one intends to see from these positions critically. . . . Self-identity is a bad visual system. . . . The split and contradictory self is the one who can interrogate positionings and be accountable. . . . I call this doubt the opening of nonisomorphic subjects, agents, and territories of stories unimaginable from the vantage point of the cyclopean, self-satiated eye of the master subject.
>
> (584–586)

Queer ethics

We want to conclude this chapter with a brief critique of the way in which museum ethics presupposes the master subject of whom Haraway is critical, and begin to articulate instead a notion of queer ethics. In the museum sector, ethics is generally understood in terms of codes of practice consisting of rational, objective principles and/or minimum standards that museum professionals are expected to be familiar with and guided by. These codes, writes Janet Marstine, are intended to professionalise practitioners by "defin[ing] appropriate behavior, establish[ing] responsibilities . . . [and] offer[ing] means for self assessment" (Marstine, 2011:7) and assessment by others. One of the problematic assumptions that underpins codes of ethics is that such codes are separate from the practitioners to whom they speak, and that their implementation is the result of conscious intent. However, as Bourdieu's account of habitus suggests, institutional(ised) idea(l)s are embodied through process of professionalisation and reproduced less-than-consciously in the actions that "make museum people" (Hakamies, 2017). In other words, codes of ethics shape those at whom they are directed, and, insofar as they are developed and implemented by museum professionals, are themselves shaped by the context in which they emerge: the relationship between museum professionals and codes of ethics is a mutually constitutive one; the two are never wholly separate. In order to be considered a professional one's practice must demonstrate the internalisation of codes of professional conduct. Adherence to the standards for professional practice outlined in codes of ethics is rewarded by a privileged position in the organisational culture of the museum (capital), and at the same time, 'dissent' – or what we might think of as 'outsider' forms of knowledge and/or practice – is equated with a lack of professionalism and may well result in censure. In other words, organisational cultures (fields) and the ways of knowing, doing, and being that subtend them (habitus) not only shape individuals, but also position them relative to one another in institutional hierarchies.

Given this, we argue for an account of ethics that recognises the constitutive relation between one's world (in this case one's professional context – the museum), one's embodied being or professional identity, one's actions or practice, and one's position relative to others in the field. As Rosalyn Diprose explains, ethics derives from the Greek word *ethos*, meaning character and dwelling or habitat. Dwelling is both a noun – the place in which I come to be (for example, it is in the context of the museum that my identity as curator is engendered and maintained) – and a verb – in this case, the practice of curating in a museum. My dwelling is both the organisational culture in which I operate, and my practice (the habitual reproduction of inherited ways of knowing, being, doing). In other words, my identity, practice, and position – or ethos as Diprose refers to it – are at once shaped by and shape the habitus in which I dwell. As such, my ethos (one's selfhood and its enactment) is always situated, relative to others, and in-process, rather than autonomous as the way of thinking that Haraway is critical of would have us believe. Ethics, from this way of thinking, is less a set of principles that a fully formed, autonomous person decides to act on (or not), than a critical practice of world-making through which we shape and are shaped.

Michel Foucault envisages ethics as a practice,

> an ethos, a philosophical life in which the critique of what we are is at one and the same time the historical analysis of the limits that are imposed on us [or, we might say, the habitus that constitutes us] and an experiment with the possibility of going beyond them.
>
> (1991:50)

Rather than assuming grounding certainties (such as the rightness of inclusion, democratic pluralism, and so on) which, as Hooper-Greenhill reminds us, may well be "tomorrow's quaint and misguided errors" (1992:10), ethics, in this sense, is queer: it is a dynamic process, an ongoing negotiation with the impossibility of ever arriving at a definitive resolution, an ideal end-point, a heaven-on-earth. Lest this should sound nihilistic, we argue, drawing on the work of Jacques Derrida (1992), that this impossibility does not render ethics redundant. Rather, it requires that instead of retreating to the security of already established moral idea(l)s and norms – an operation which, as Derrida would see it, is mechanical, perfunctory, and empty of ethical content – we rise to the ethical challenge of thinking beyond what we (think we) know, to being open to ways of knowing, being, doing, that may not be immediately intelligible to us. In other words, rather than simply arguing for the inclusion of LGBTIQ+ his/stories, practices, modes of being, in order to redress past imbalances, or suggesting that we replace an oppressive model of museological practice with a liberatory one, we advocate a troubling of the categorical logic that underpins these kinds of claims. In doing so we want to avoid what Bradburne describes as the tendency, common in museums, "to become locked in the perverse logic of representation"; to replace " '[b]ad' old grand narratives" with " 'good' new decentered" ones, to "make museums of victims" rather than "of heroes", to "make museums that trumpet new identities" instead of museums that "celebrate imperial identity" (2011:276). Instead, we offer up the challenge of ongoing critique, of relinquishing certainty in the name of queer ethics.

Notes

1 Hooper-Greenhill uses this Foucauldian term to refer to beliefs and ways of thinking that are taken as self-evident and not in need of explanation (1992:3–4).
2 The term 'subaltern' was coined by Antonio Gramsci in his work on cultural hegemony and refers to populations that are excluded by the hegemonic power structures of the colony and thus denied a voice. Gayatri Spivak (1998), uses this term to refer to non-Western others whose ways of knowing are relegated to the margins of intellectual discourse by being constructed as myth and/or folklore. To be heard and known, the subaltern must adopt Western ways of knowing, of thought, reasoning, and language.
3 For an extended account of this claim, see Ahmed (2007).
4 While acknowledging the merits of and motivations behind the *Proud Nation Survey* – the aim of which was to construct a database of LGBT-related holdings in GLAM institutions in the UK – it is worth simultaneously pointing out that the project is founded on the problematic assumption that queer objects are self-evidently so. It also fails to consider that what makes an object 'queer' (or available to queer practice) might have more to do with interpretation than with essence.
5 Laenui is drawing here on the work of Filipino psychologist Virgilio G. Enriquez.
6 See Marchia and Sommer (2017) for a more detailed account.
7 'Cisgender' is a term for people whose gender identity matches the sex that they were assigned at birth. It is, as Jessica Cadwallader explains, "a way of drawing attention to the unmarked norm, against which trans is identified" (2009:17).
8 Practice, as Inkeri Hakamies puts it, "makes 'museum people'" (2017:142).

9 On the very rare occasion that our museum would collect a sculpture it would be because it has some historical significance not because it is a noteworthy work of art.
10 Bourdieu (1984) refers to these people as taste makers.
11 Consequently, institutions such as museums tend to employ the same 'types' of people and to exclude 'others', rather than interrogating their own assumptions/biases, opening themselves up to others and thus to other ways of knowing and doing. See Kinsley (2016) for discussion of the kinds of initiatives that some institutions have introduced in an attempt to diversify the workforce.
12 See Bell et al. (1994) for discussion of the claim that space is always already sexed, gendered, and so on.
13 We use this term in an attempt to gesture towards the 'non-normative' while at the same time, avoiding applying contemporary concepts and labels to identities, practices, and relationships that were experienced, expressed, and understood in contextually specific ways that may no longer be available to us, or that may not ever have applied in other cultural contexts. For an interesting discussion of the process of decision-making regarding the use of terminology in a contemporary exhibition on a historic practice, see Ikeda (2018).
14 We have deliberately left out 'I' here because we are unaware of any attempts made by museums to engage with intersex.
15 Grand narrative is a term introduced by Jean-François Lyotard in his classic work *The Postmodern Condition: A Report on Knowledge* (1979). Lyotard argues that what we perceive as truth is constructed as such in and through universalising accounts – or grand narratives – of subjectivity and sociality that govern particular cultures at particular times. One such narrative embraces the notion of human being (and of history) as evolving towards an enlightened or ideal state of being. As a result, actions, artworks, scientific 'discoveries', particular lifestyles, and so on, are judged on the basis of whether or not they supposedly contribute to, or inhibit, such progress. Lyotard and other poststructuralist theorists are critical of grand narratives because they leave no room for difference, for complexities, or for ambiguity.
16 Drawing on what has been claimed to be one of the founding texts of queer theory, Eve Kosofsky's *Epistemology of the Closet* (1990), Mills uses this term to refer to (and critique) the binary logic that is characteristic of Western modernity, and, in particular, the assumption that self-revelation and recognition are unproblematic and liberatory. For a detailed critique of liberation through self-revelation and the 'repressive hypothesis' that subtends it, see Foucault (1980).
17 Matt Smith's curatorial intervention *Piccadilly 1830* at Nymans House and Gardens in East Sussex, UK, queers heterornormative temporality in really interesting ways. Smith's intervention focusses on Oliver Mussel, one of three siblings who lived with their parents at Nymans House in the early twentieth century, and whose relationship with Vagn Riis-Hansen is not, as his sibling's intimate relationships are, discussed in the property's guidebook *The Nymans Story*. Instead, the guidebook focusses on Oliver's career as a theatre and interior designer. Inspired by a highlander costume held at the V & A which Messel designed for Serge Lifar to wear in a dance piece called *Piccadilly 1830*, which formed part of Charles Cochran's stage production entitled *1930 Revue*, and which "compressed two dates into one location – the Piccadilly of 1830 as a haunt for upper-class men" and the 1930s cruising ground for "working-class

Dilly boys" (Smith, 2017:108), Smith created an installation that likewise weaves together past and present and creates a space for difference to exist. The installation which explored the fragility of performances of masculinity consisted of a sculpture entitled *The Antique Youth*, whose nose and genitals are missing, bedecked in an oversized ostrich feather bearskin and a military-style jacket that Smith made and embellished with thousands of mirror-backed glass beads. For a more detailed account of this and other similar interventions, see Smith (2017).

18 See Talburt and Matus (2012) for a critique of the appropriation of penguins in homonormative narratives.

19 Similarly, Michael Warner argues that queer "rejects a minoritizing logic of toleration or simple political interest-representation in favor of a more thorough resistance to regimes of the normal" (1993:xxvi).

20 Hooper-Greenhill uses this term in the Foucauldian sense to refer to "the unconscious but positive and productive set of relations within which knowledge is produced and rationality defined" (1992:12).

21 The notion of a diffractive optics as a way of seeing that queers or disorients heteronormative optics is discussed at length by Haraway (2004c).

22 Sandra Harding asserts that feminist researchers should appear not as the "invisible, anonymous, disembodied voice of authority, but as . . . real historical individuals[s] with concrete, specific desires and interests" (1987:9). In Chapter 3 we address some of the ways in which curatorial positionality might be acknowledged and made visible to others.

References

Adair, J. (2017). O [Queer] Pioneers! Narrating Queer Lives in Virtual Museums. *Museum & Society*, 15(2), 114–125.

Ahmed, S. (2007). 'You End Up Doing the Document Rather Than Doing the Doing': Diversity, Race Equality and the Politics of Documentation. *Ethnic and Racial Studies*, 30(4), 590–609.

Ahmed, S. (2006). *Queer Phenomenology: Orientations, Objects, Others*. Durham: Duke University Press.

Barnard, I. (1999). Queer Race. *Social Semiotics*, 9(2), 199–212.

Bell, D., Binnie, J., Cream, J., & Valentine, G. (1994). All Hyped Up and No Place to Go. *Gender Place & Culture*, 1(1), 31–47.

Bennett, T. (1995). *The Birth of the Museum*. London: Routledge.

Berlant, L., & Warner, M. (1998). Sex in Public. *Critical Inquiry*, 24(2), 547–566.

Bosold, B., & Hofmann, V. (2018). A Special Place in Hell: Reflections on Current Programming Strategies of Schwules Museum Berlin. In J. Katz, I. Hufschmidt, & A. Söll (Eds.), *Queer Curating*, a special issue of *On Curating*, 37, 5–12.

Bourdieu, P. (1998). *Acts of Resistance: Against the Myths of Our Time*. Cambridge: Polity Press.

Bourdieu, P. (1984). *Distinction: A Social Critique of the Judgement of Taste*. London: Routledge.

Bourdieu, P. (1980). *The Logic of Practice*. Stanford, CA: Stanford University Press.

Bradburne, J. (2011). Visible Listening: Discussion, Debate and Governance in the Museum. In J. Marstine (Ed.), *The Routledge Companion to Museum Ethics* (pp. 275–284). London: Routledge.

Butler, J. (1993/2011). *Bodies That Matter: On the Discursive Limits of "Sex"*. New York: Routledge.

Cadwallader, J. (2009). Diseased States: The Role of Pathology in the (Re)Production of the Body Politic. In N. Sullivan & S. Murray (Eds.), *Somatechnics: Queering the Technologisation of Bodies* (pp. 13–28). Farnham: Ashgate.

Cassidy, A., Lock, S., & Voss, G. (2016). Sexual Nature? (Re)presenting Sexuality and Science in the Museum. *Science as Culture*, 25(2), 214–238.

Communities, Sport and Recreation, Department of Premier and Cabinet. (2015). *Whole-of-Government Framework for Lesbian, Gay, Bisexual, Transgender and Intersex Tasmanians*. Hobart: CSRDPC.

Conlan, A. (2010). Representing Possibility: Mourning, Memorial and Queer Museology. In A. K. Levin (Ed.), *Gender, Sexuality and Museums: A Routledge Reader* (pp. 253–263). London and New York: Routledge.

Crenshaw, K. (1991). Mapping the Margins: Intersectionality, Identity Politics, and Violence Against Women of Color. *Stanford Law Review*, 43(6), 1241–1299.

Curtain, B. (2018). The Terms of Visibility: Between Queer and LGBT in Curating Art in Asia. *On Curating*, 37, 13–21.

Department for Communities and Social Inclusion, Government of South Australia. (2014). *South Australian Strategy for the Inclusion of Lesbian, Gay, Bisexual, Transgender, Intersex and Queer People 2014–2016*. Adelaide: DCSI.

Department of Culture, Media and Sports. (2005). *Understanding the Future: Museums and 21st Century*. London: DCMS.

Department of Culture, Media and Sports. (2000a). *Centres for Social Change: Museums, Galleries and Archives for All*. London: DCMS.

Department of Culture, Media and Sports. (2000b). *The Learning Power of Museums: A Vision for Museum Education*. London: DCMS.

Department of Culture, Media and Sports. (1999). *Museums for the Many: Standards for Museums and Galleries to Use When Developing Access Policies*. London: DCMS.

Department of Premier and Cabinet, Victorian State Government. (2016). *LGBTI Inclusion Plan 2016–2017*. Melbourne: DPC.

Dewdney, A., Dibosa, D., & Walsh, V. (2012). Cultural Diversity: Politics, Policy and Practices. The Case of Tate Encounters. In R. Sandell & E. Nightingale (Eds.), *Museums, Equality and Social Justice* (pp. 114–124). London and New York: Routledge.

Duggan, L. (2004). The New Homonormativity: The Sexual Politics of Neoliberalism. In R. Csatronovo & D. Nelson (Eds.), *Materializing Democracy: Toward a Revitalized Cultural Politics* (pp. 175–194). Durham: Duke University Press.

Duggan, L. (1992). Making it Perfectly Queer. *Socialist Review*, 22(1), 11–31.

Emirbayer, M., & Johnson, V. (2008). Bourdieu and Organizational Analysis. *Theory and Society*, 37(1), 1–44.

Fleming, D. (2016). Do Museums Change Lives? Ninth Stephen Weil Memorial Lecture. *Curator: The Museum Journal*, 59(2), 73–79.

Foucault, M. (2005/1966). *The Order of Things: An Archaeology of the Human Sciences*. London and New York: Routledge.

Foucault, M. (1991). What Is Enlightenment? In P. Rabinow (Ed.), *The Foucault Reader* (pp. 32–50). Harmondsworth: Penguin.

Foucault, M. (1980). *The History of Sexuality Volume 1: An Introduction*. New York: Vintage Books.

Frost, S. (2015). Museums and Sexuality. *Museum International*, 65(1–4), 16–25.

Hakamies, I. (2017). Practice Makes "Museum People". *Museum & Society*, 15(2), 142–152.

Haraway, D. (2004a). Introduction: A Kinship of Feminist Figurations. In D. Haraway (Ed.), *The Haraway Reader* (pp. 1–6). New York and London: Routledge.

Haraway, D. (2004b). Teddy Bear Patriarchy: Taxidermy in the Garden of Eden, New York City, 1908–1936. In D. Haraway (Ed.), *The Haraway Reader* (pp. 151–198). New York and London: Routledge.

Haraway, D. (2004c). The Promise of Monsters: A Regenerative Politics for Inappropriate/d Others. In D. Haraway (Ed.), *The Haraway Reader* (pp. 63–44). New York and London: Routledge.

Haraway, D. (1988). Situated Knowledges: The Science Question in Feminism and the Privilege of Partial Perspective. *Feminist Studies*, 14(3), 575–599.

Harding, S. (1987). Introduction: Is There A Feminist Method? In S. Harding (Ed.), *Feminist Methodology* (pp. 1–14). Bloomington: Indiana University Press.

Hooper-Greenhill, E. (1992). *Museums and the Shaping of Knowledge*. London: Routledge.

Hufschmidt, I. (2018). The Queer Institutional, Or How to Inspire Queer Curating. In J. Katz, I. Hufschmidt, & A. Söll (Eds.), *Queer Curating*, a special issue of *On Curating*, 37, 29–32.

Ikeda, A. (2018). Curating A Third Gender: Beautiful Youths in Japanese Prints. *Transgender Studies Quarterly*, 5(4), 638–647.

Iverson, S. V. (2007). Camouflaging Power and Privilege: A Critical Race Analysis of University Diversity Policies. *Educational Administration Quarterly*, 43(5), 586–611.

Kinsley, R. P. (2016). Inclusion in Museums: A Matter of Social Justice. *Museum Management and Curatorship*, 31(5), 474–490.

Laenui, P. (2006). *Processes of Decolonization*. www.sjsu.edu/people/marcos.pizarro/maestros/Laenui.pdf. Accessed December 1, 2018.

Leahy, H. R. (2012). *Museum Bodies: The Politics and Practices of Visiting and Viewing*. London: Routledge.

Levin, A. (2012). Unpacking Gender: Creating Complex Models for Gender Inclusivity. In R. Sandell & E. Nightingale (Eds.), *Museums, Equality and Social Justice* (pp. 156–168). London and New York: Routledge.

Liddiard, M. (2004). Changing Histories: Museums, Sexuality and the Future of the Past. *Museums and Society*, 2(1), 15–29.

Lyotard, J-F. (1979/1984). *The Postmodern Condition: A Report on Knowledge*. Manchester: Manchester University Press.

Macdonald, S. (1998). Exhibitions of Power and Powers of Exhibition: An Introduction to the Politics of Display. In S. Macdonald (Ed.), *The Politics of Display: Museums, Science, Culture* (pp. 1–24). London: Routledge.

Marchia, J., & Sommer, J. M. (2017). (Re)defining Heteronormativity. *Sexualities*, 22(3), 267–295.

Marstine, J. (2011). The Contingent Nature of the New Museum Ethics. In J. Marstine (Ed.), *The Routledge Companion to Museum Ethics* (pp. 3–25). London: Routledge.

Message, K. (2013). Slipping Through the Cracks: Museums and Social Inclusion in Australian Cultural Policy Development 2007–10. *International Journal of Cultural Policy*, 19(2), 201–221.

Millard, R. (2011). London Museum Goes Wild with Animal Sex Exhibit. *Sydney Morning Herald*, February 11. www.smh.com.au/world/london-museum-goes-wild-with-animal-sex-exhibit-20110211-1aov1.html. Accessed November 5, 2015.

Mills, R. (2010). Queer Is Here? Lesbian, Gay, Bisexual and Transgender Histories and Public Culture. In A. K. Levin (Ed.), *Gender, Sexuality and Museums: A Routledge Reader* (pp. 80–88). London and New York: Routledge.

Mills, R. (2008). Theorizing the Queer Museum. *Museums & Social Issues*, 3(1), 41–52.

Mollow, A., & McRuer, R. (2012). Introduction. In A Mollow & R. McRuer (Eds.), *Sex and Disability* (pp. 1–34). Durham: Duke University Press.

Muñiz-Reed, I. (2017). Thoughts on Curatorial Practices in the Decolonial Turn. *On Curating*, 35, 99–105.

Muňoz, J. E. (1999). *Disidentifications: Queers of Color and the Performance of Politics*. Minneapolis and London: University of Minnesota Press.

Nightingale, E., & Sandell, R. (2012). Introduction. In R. Sandell & E. Nightingale (Eds.), *Museums, Equality and Social Justice* (pp. 1–9). London: Routledge.

Nochlin, L. (1971/1989). Why Have There Been No Great Women Artists? *Women, Art and Power and Other Essays* (pp. 145–179). London: Thames and Hudson.

O'Neill, M. (2002). The Good Enough Visitor. In R. Sandell (Ed.), *Museums, Society, Inequality* (pp. 24–40). London: Routledge.

Parker, R., & Pollock, G. (1981). *Old Mistresses: Women, Art, and Ideology*. London: Routledge and Kegan Paul.

Piper, A. (1996/2003). The Triple Negation of Colored Women Artists. In A. Jones (Ed.), *The Feminism and Visual Culture Reader* (pp. 239–248). London: Routledge.

Public Service Commission, State of Queensland. (2017). *Queensland Public Sector LGBTIQ+ Inclusion Strategy*. Brisbane: PSC.

Robert, N. (2014). Getting Intersectional in Museums. *Museums and Social Issues*, 9(1), 24–33.

Sandell, R. (2017). *Museums, Moralities and Human Rights*. London: Routledge.

Sandell, R. (2003). Social Inclusion, the Museum and the Dynamics of Sectoral Change. *Museum and Society*, 1(1), 45–62.

Saunders, J. (2008). The Museum's Silent Sexual Performance. *Museums & Social Issues*, 3(1), 15–28.

Sedgwick, E. K. (1990). *Epistemology of the Closet*. Berkeley: University of California Press.

Sentance, N. (2018). Diversity Means Disruption. *Archival Decolonist [-o-]*, November 28. https://archivaldecolonist.com/

Smith, M. (2017). Queering the Historic House: Destabilizing Heteronormativity in the National Trust. In B. Pilkey, R. M. Scicluna, B. Campkin, & B. Penner (Eds.), *Sexuality and Gender at Home: Experience, Politics, Transgression* (pp. 105–120). London: Bloomsbury Academic.

Smith, M., & Sandell, R. (2018). Bringing Queer Home. In R. Sandell, R. Lennon, & M. Smith (Eds.), *Prejudice and Pride: LGBTQ Heritage and its Contemporary Implications* (pp. 38–49). Leicester: Research Centre for Museums and Galleries, University of Leicester.

Spivak, G. C. (1988). Can the Subaltern Speak? In C. Nelson & L. Grossberg (Eds.), *Marxism and the Interpretation of Culture* (pp. 271–313). Urbana, IL: University of Illinois Press.

Steorn, P. (2012). Curating Queer Heritage: Queer Knowledge and Museum Practice. *Digital*, 55(3), 355–365.

Sullivan, N. (2003). *A Critical Introduction to Queer Theory*. Edinburgh: Edinburgh University Press.

Sullivan, N., & Middleton, C. (2019). Warning! Heteronormativity: A Question of Ethics. In A. Levin & J. Adair (Eds.), *Museums, Sexuality, and Gender Activism*.

Swinney, G. (2012). What do we know about what we know? The Museum "register" as Museum Object. In S. Dudley, A. J. Barners, J. Binnie, J. Petrou, & J. Walklate (Eds.), *The Thing About Museums: Objects and Experience, Representation and Contestation* (pp. 31–46). London and New York: Routledge.

Talburt, S., & Matus, C. (2012). Orienting Ourselves to the Gay Penguin. *Journal of Emotion, Space and Society*, 5(1), 36–44.

Taylor, C. (1994). The Politics of Recognition. In A. Gutman (Ed.), *Multiculturalism: Examining the Politics of Recognition* (pp. 25–74). Princeton, NJ: Princeton University Press.

Tyburczy, J. (2016). *Sex Museums: The Politics and Performance of Display*. Chicago: University of Chicago Press.

Tyburczy, J. (2014). Leather Anatomy: Cripping Homonormativity at International Mr Leather. *Journal of Literary & Cultural Disability Studies*, 8(3), 275–293.

Wacquant, L. (2005). Habitus. In J. Becket & M. Zafirovski (Eds.), *International Encyclopedia of Economic Sociology* (pp. 315–319). London: Routledge.

Wallis, B. (2003). Black Bodies, White Science: Louis Agassiz's Slave Daguerreotypes. In C. Fusco & B. Wallis (Eds.), *Only Skin Deep: Changing Visions of the American Self* (pp. 163–182). New York: Harry N. Abrams Inc.

Warner, M. (1993). Introduction. In M. Warner (Ed.), *Fear of A Queer Planet: Queer Politics and Social Theory* (pp. vii–xxxi). Minneapolis: University of Minnesota Press.

Watson, S. (2009). Myth, Memory and the Senses in the Churchill Museum. In S. Dudley (Ed.), *Museum Materialities: Objects, Engagements, Interpretations* (pp. 204–223). London: Routledge.

White, B. E. (1976). A 1974 Perspective: Why Women's Studies in Art and Art History? *Art Journal*, 35(4), 340–344.

Winchester, O. (2012). A Book With Its Pages Always Open?. In E. Nightingale & R. Sandell (Eds.), *Museums, Equality and Social Justice* (pp. 124–155). London: Routledge.

2 Queer/ing display

Museums orient us in the world: they offer us ways to think, paths to follow, object lessons, and narrative positions with which to identify. And they do this through the careful staging of what is seen and what is felt (Tyburczy, 2016:7). As many scholars before us have argued, exhibition-making is a professionalised practice involving an array of learned structural conventions and techniques particular to a given habitus (Fleming, 2010; Moser, 2010; Thomas, 2010; Tyburczy, 2016; Vogel, 1991), none of which are neutral or natural (Sandell, 2007:195). The uncritical reiteration of conventional display techniques (such as those associated with object selection and arrangement, labelling, exhibition layout) can, as we saw in the previous chapter, (re)produce "taxonomies of normalcy" which, through their repetition, "take on the force of the natural" (Tyburczy, 2016:11). At the same time, it can render alternative ways of knowing and being less viable. As Oliver Winchester puts it,

> A museum's potential to explain is always based on its ability to focus on a particular set of relations and meanings between objects. . . . [P]roblematic, superfluous or redundant associations are dismissed in favour of a predetermined script, thus ensuring the delivery of a singular, coherent . . . intellectual narrative. . . . [T]hese narratives are always predicated upon exclusions.
>
> (2012:142)

Insofar as display contributes to world-making,[1] it, like the practitioners who compose "the museum as a meaning-making machine" (Winchester, 2012:153), is implicated in the "organiz[ation] and co-ordinat[ion of] an order of things and . . . produce[s] a place for people in relation to that order" (Bennett, 1988:80). And, as we demonstrated in the previous chapter, heteronormativity – as an order(ing) of things and people – is, by definition, inequitable. Given this, we repeat the call made by Martha Fleming to pay more attention to *how* meaning is made (to how *we* make meaning), to acknowledge that museological practice is a form of scholarship whose methods can be extrapolated, critically interrogated, and reconfigured (2010:35). This chapter, then, offers some thoughts on and examples of what Jennifer Tyburczy calls queer curatorship. Queer curatorship, she writes, is, amongst other things, "a mode for putting queer theory on its feet"; it is

> simultaneously a mode for studying how museums place objects in normative sexual relationships through the curatorial citation and repetition of familiar arrangements, juxtapositions, and chronologies, and a method for experimenting with object arrangements toward the cultivation of other sexual-social relationships.
>
> (Tyburczy, 2016:199)

Moving beyond absence/presence

In the previous chapter we noted that while an increasing number of museums and galleries have, in the last couple of decades, turned their attention to LGBTIQ+ his/stories, identities, lives, and works, such things nevertheless remain largely absent in mainstream institutions globally. We also suggested that the predominant response to this absence has been to argue that LGBTIQ+ inclusion and visibility are matters of social justice to which museums have a moral responsibility to respond. The effects of such assertions have been mixed: on the one hand (some) previously ignored communities, histories, and practices have made their way into museums – even if, for the most part, temporarily – but on the other, representation in the space of the museum has all too often meant the reproduction of heteronormative logic and idea(l)s. To represent, as the term suggests, is to re-present, to make present that which is absent (in this case LGBTIQ+ lives). The assumption underlying calls for LGBTIQ+ representation is that LGBTIQ+ identity and/or history is fully formed, definable, and separate from and not affected by representational practices. This has led to the production of exhibitions that are problematic in at least two connected senses. First, most LGBTIQ+ exhibitions have focussed disproportionately on white, cisgender, able-bodied men, and in doing so have failed to critically interrogate the ways in which notions of gender and sexuality are culturally constructed in contextually specific ways and in relation to other vectors of identity – in particular race, class, ability, and so on. Second, and as such, rather than experimenting with the possibility of moving beyond heteronormative ways of knowing, being and doing, the additive approach to inclusion has invariably replaced one set of exclusions with another (Levin, 2012:158–159).

How else, then, might we respond to the absences that so many of us understandably bemoan? Steven Lubar (2018) suggests that rather than attempting to overcome absence we might instead call attention to it in order to raise questions about the role that museums play in the (re)production of identity and difference, systems of power and privilege, and past, present, and future inequalities. For us, one of the most powerful examples of this approach is Fred Wilson's seminal intervention *Mining the Museum* which took place at the Maryland Historical Society (MHS) in 1992–1993. In particular, the 'Truth Trophy' installation that visitors encountered on first entering the exhibition space exemplifies what we might think of as a queering of absence and its epistemological underpinnings. The display consisted of three elements. The first, a silver-plated globe embossed with the word TRUTH that had been awarded to advertising agencies in the first decades of the twentieth century for 'truth in advertising', was displayed in an acrylic case along with eight (tellingly) empty miniature plinths. Flanking the case were two sets of three pedestals. Those on the left were empty except for a small plaque bearing the names of influential African-American Marylanders (Harriet Tubman, Frederick Douglass, and Benjamin Banneker),[2] while those on the right supported the busts of Henry Clay, Napoleon Bonaparte, and Andrew Jackson, three white men generally thought to have little or no connection to Maryland. Rachel Smith, however, claims that Jackson and Clay "were members of the American Colonization Society, which was responsible for establishing a colony called Maryland in Liberia for the purposes of forcefully removing the free black population of the state" (2014:13). As such the men's historical relationship to the state of Maryland is one based on racism rather than geographic proximity. Bearing this in mind, writes Smith, "the narrative of the Maryland Historical Society seems to be complicit with a history of racism, and the silences constructed by the archive seem even more egregious" (2014:13).

Rather than simply including African-Americans in the MHS, Wilson at once deployed and put a twist on recognisable curatorial tools and conventions (the vitrine, the placing of busts on classical pedestals, symmetry, juxtaposition, standardised labels, lighting, and so on) in order "to show how a slight adjustment in emphasis or subject can expose the museum's point of view" (Wilson & Berger, 2011:155), its biases, and blind spots. In particular, the juxtaposition of incongruous elements – the truth globe, and two sets of plinths (one empty) – thwarts the viewer's expectations, and opens up space for what Wilson describes as a "third thought": "It is my thought" says Wilson, "but it allows the viewer to enter into my thinking a bit, but come up with conclusions for themselves, as well" (2011a:279). For us, 'Truth Trophy' exposes the museological technologies through which histories are constructed and, through their repetition, take on the status of truth. But perhaps more important still, it makes literal and visible what Judith Butler refers to as "the exclusionary matrix by which subjects are formed" (1999:236): the empty plinths (standing in for the excluded, for, in Butlerian terms, those who do not enjoy the status of the subject) representationally support a very particular view of history, progress, 'civilisation', one epitomised by the figure of 'man'/the subject by serving as its counterpoint. This figure is at once, as the busts imply, both universal and particular – that is, white, able-bodied, cisgender, affluent, and so on. What Wilson demonstrates in 'Truth Trophy' is that "the subject is constituted through the force of exclusion and abjection, one which produces . . . an abjected outside, which is, after all, 'inside' the subject as its own founding repudiation" (Butler, 1999:237). In doing so Wilson both reveals and challenges the museological mechanisms – in particular the assumption of a detached and neutral point of observation from which the museum maps and classifies the world that Santaigo Castro-Gómez refers to as the "hubris of the zero point" (2005) – by which such inequalities are perpetuated. Today, writes Walter Mignolo, "that assumption is no longer tenable, although there are still many believers" (2009:1).

More recently Ashkan Sepahvand curated an exhibition (featuring the work of 16 artists) and symposium at the Schwules* Museum[3] in Berlin[4] entitled *Odarodle: an imaginary their_story of naturepeoples, 1535–2017*, which aimed to queer the colonial underpinnings of the museum and its ongoing impact on exhibitionary practice.[5] The origins of the Schwules* Museum (established in 1985) can be traced back to an exhibition about the history of lesbian and gay lives and communities in Berlin, held at Märkisches Museum in 1984 and entitled *Eldorado*. As Sepahvand explains, the title, *Eldorado*, referred to a cabaret club and queer haunt that operated (in various venues) during Berlin's 'golden years' (1910s – early 1930s), and to the legendary 'lost city of gold' that, like other such fantasies, fueled Europe's imperial race for wealth, power, and territory in the sixteenth, seventeenth, and eighteenth centuries. *Odarodle* – Eldorado backwards – queers these three interconnected 'myths' and the role they have played in the construction of cultural fictions of the 'other'. Sepahvand describes the *Eldorado* exhibition as an attempt to create a grand narrative which was at once didactic, encyclopaedic, objective, ethnographic, and intended to educate a 'genuinely interested' liberal, bourgeois audience. While the representation and recognition of homosexuality that *Eldorado* set out to achieve was and, for many, continues to be, a step in the right political direction, from the post-colonial perspective that Sepahvand inhabits the approach is problematic in its construction of homosexuals as ethnographic specimens whose being becomes the object of knowledge for the (presumably white, cisgender, middle-class) subject of knowledge whose subjectivity and ways of knowing are thereby reaffirmed.[6]

Both the layout of *Odarodle* and the various displays that compose it critically engaged with the politics of representation and worked to queer the epistemological foundation of *Eldorado* and its ongoing influence. Of most interest to us is the ‘Welcome Address’ that visitors encountered on entering the gallery. Itself an artwork (although, at first glance, not obviously so) by Vika Kirchenbauer, ‘Welcome Address’, features Sepahvand wearing a T-shirt emblazoned with the words “Community & Diversity Day” (Figure 2.1),[7] and speaking in a fictionalised first-person voice authored by Kirchenbauer.[8]

The piece opens with Sepahvand speaking the following (somewhat cliched) words: “Hello. Please let me welcome you. Everybody is welcome”. He then introduces himself and explains that his position in the museum was made possible by a grant from the German Federal Cultural Foundation awarded to the Schwules* Museum for a project which, for the first time, brings a post-colonial perspective to bear on the museum’s collection and history. Sepahvand then welcomes visitors again and goes on to state “I am a queer person of colour and I identify primarily as an artistic researcher. In fact, I’m flattered to be on display as well as to display. Welcome. If I am welcome here then so are you”. Rather than offering a smooth entry into the exhibition, ‘Welcome Address’ disorients: one is unsure – particularly initially – how to read it: is it genuine, exaggerated, mocking,

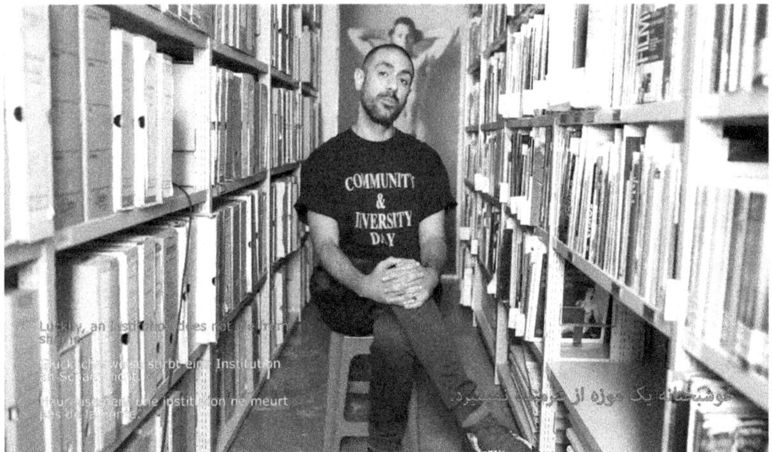

Figure 2.1 Sepahvand in T-shirt

© Vika Kirchenbauer and VG Bild Kunst 6

tokenistic, cynical? And how might one 'know'? Disorientation, writes Sara Ahmed, "makes things oblique, which, in turn, opens up another way to inhabit" (2006:569) the normative forms that orient us: what is familiar – in this case, the discourse of diversity and inclusion – is made strange.[9] Indeed, 'Welcome Address' "expose[s] a public secret": that is, that "prized, progressive notions such as difference and diversity readily transform into a form of symbolic currency . . . bartered between cultural practitioners, funding bodies, and target audiences" (Sepahvand, 2017:npn), and that those performing the labour of institutional critique often trade on their 'otherness' in order to gain opportunities that allow them to carry out such work.

Whether our awareness of this process of tactically deploying what Sepahvand refers to as a "general politically correct turn within cultural representation based on filling quotas without necessarily challenging the systemic inequalities that maintain the norm", is wholly or less-than conscious, "we act as if it were not the case". What 'Welcome Address' does instead is to offer a performance of institutional critique in which the critic is shown to be at once at a critical distance from and implicated in the institution and the discourses that inform it.[10] This is made obvious when Sepahvand turns around and the viewer sees the word "Staff" on the back of his T-shirt (Figure 2.2). In other words, rather than responding to the absence of non-white lives and histories in the Schwules* Museum by uncritically insisting on their inclusion (which would constitute an assimilation of 'otherness' into a colonial framework for knowing and being) 'Welcome Address', and

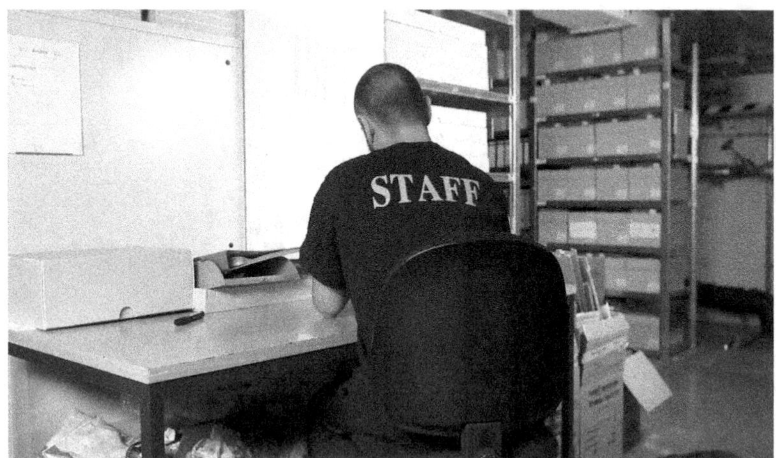

Figure 2.2 Sepahvand from behind

Credit: © Vika Kirchenbauer and VG Bild Kunst 4

Odarodle more broadly, exposes the contradictions and complexities of the politics of representation, and the ways in which we, as practitioners, museum visitors, activists, and so on, are (necessarily, albeit differently) implicated in their re/de/construction.

Object lessons in disorderly conduct

One of the justifications regularly given for not including LGBTIQ+ content in museums is a (perceived) lack of objects. But if, as 'Truth Trophy' suggests,[11] it is not necessary to display 'African-American' objects in order to explore histories of racialisation and/or racism in the USA, then to what extent do we need LGBTIQ+ objects in order to perform similar interventions? And what constitutes an LGBTIQ+ object anyway? We will briefly address the latter question later in the chapter, but for now we turn to *The Gay Museum*, an exhibition held at the Western Australian Museum (WAM) in 2003, which has been the source of much inspiration for us. *The Gay Museum* was the outcome of a PhD project in which artist Jo Darbyshire set out to explore the history of LGBT presence and identity in Western Australia, and, at the same time, to critically reflect on practices of meaning-making. In response to the absence of LGBT objects in WAM's collection[12] and of LGBT his/stories and lives in museums more generally, Darbyshire used a range of "creative interpretation strategies" (2003a:15) – including recontextualisation, juxtaposition, disjunction, parody, non-linear multiple narratives, temporal transgressions, repetition, visual metaphors, and text as a visual medium[13] – to open up meaning (rather than insisting on its singularity and fixedness) and encourage self-reflexivity about the role that visitors, and those who produce exhibitions, play in the (re)production of heteronormative ways of knowing and being. Moreover, as the following examples show, Darbyshire's approach set out to challenge some of the 'unspoken rules' that structure museological practice. These include the connected beliefs that "objects with no provenance should not be displayed", that "only the best examples should be shown" and that "objects should be exhibited in the same way they are classified – to show function or provenance, or, in the case of natural history artefacts, their scientific place in an order" (Darbyshire, 2003a:72–73).

The shoe ashtray and the shame-faced crab displays both exemplify how the de/re/contextualisation of collection objects and their juxtaposition with text from other mediums and conceptual registers, and other historical moments, opens up space for the proliferation of meanings. Darbyshire tells how, whilst rummaging in WAM's history department warehouse she found "a small, elegant silver shoe, produced in the 1930s or 40s, which contained a hidden ashtray". For the artist, the object immediately referenced "a 'social style' or fetish" (2003a:68) that its functional categorisation as 'ashtray' at best overlooked and at worst, denied. Rather than ignoring the object's function, Darbyshire's aesthetic approach[14] also foregrounded other elements and connections by juxtaposing the dainty, highly-stylised shoe with "text that gave a definition of the word Fag – a derogatory term for a homosexual man that originated in the 1920s, when smoking cigarettes was seen to be effeminate compared to smoking cigars" (2003a:69). Similarly, the "provocative juxtaposition" (Mills, 2008:49) of the *Calappa philargius*, or shame-faced crab (Figure 2.3) as it is more colloquially known,[15] with a quote from Geoffrey Davis, a member of CAMP (Campaign Against Moral Persecution), one of Australia's first gay rights activist groups, in which he decries the destruction of CAMP's records when the group disbanded in 1988,[16] encourages viewers to speculate about the role and function of categorisation, shame, fear of persecution, and hiding and exposure in the construction of history and identity. Interestingly, the initial resistance of natural history curators to displaying an item from their collection in what they perceived to be a social history exhibition, to making 'improper associations' and thereby risking 'losing face', adds another dimension to such speculations.

Darbyshire's queer tactics also included importing what might be regarded as insignificant and/or improper objects into the exhibition in order to invoke meanings and connections through the use of visual metaphor. In one display she juxtaposed an electroconvulsive therapy machine[17]

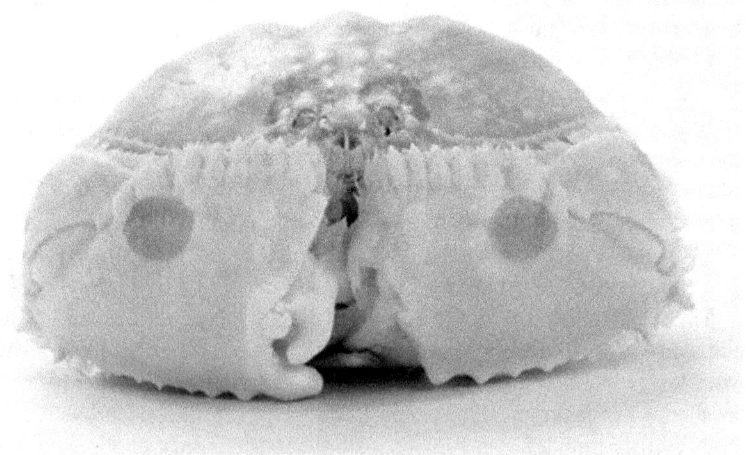

Figure 2.3 A shame-faced crab

Credit: Courtesy Jo Darbyshire, the Gay Museum, WA Museum, 2003.

with 60 pieces[18] of used soap, and text about 'cures' for homosexuality, thus provoking viewers to consider how seemingly mundane, repetitious practices (such as those associated with hygiene), the idea(l)s with which they are connected (for example, cleanliness, health, wellbeing, propriety), and the emotional affects to which they adhere (guilt, shame, repugnance, virtuousness) contribute (both historically and in the present) to the reproduction of heteronormativity, social inequality, and symbolic and actual violence. Rather than offering a linear account of a shift from the bad old days of homosexual oppression to the enlightened present, the display at once showcases historic abuses and the knowledges that inform them, draws attention to the problematics of the repetition of habituated, taken-for-granted practices (including display practices), and performatively opens up sexual pasts, presents, and futures to alternative configurations.

Drawing on and citing Leigh Summers' work on bodily fluids and the sanitisation of bodies and histories in social history museums, Darbyshire also displayed a pair of 1950s men's woollen bathers that had been donated but not accessioned because the "icky" stain on the crotch made them – at least in the eyes of one curator – "too disgusting to display" (cited in Darbyshire, 2003a:74–75). For Darbyshire on the other hand, this trace of what, according to the mores of the museum, cannot be articulated, disordered the classificatory focus on function and/or provenance and enabled other, more speculative meanings and connections to emerge – between male bodies, pleasure, homosociality, physique culture and clothing, and beachside beats.[19] If, as Jennifer Tyburczy (2016) has argued, museums have established taxonomies of ab/normalcy through the ubiquitous display of some ways of knowing, being, and doing, and the exclusion of those considered (and thus constructed as) 'obscene', then Darbyshire's display of what we want to think of, following Herring, as "disordered/disordering materiality", both exposes and destablises the heteronormativity of the 'normal', the "regulatory mechanisms that are deployed to disallow or to disavow certain human attachments . . . and to promote others" (Terry cited in Herring, 2011:npn). Rather than including 'the gay man' (as a fully formed and knowable figure) into a heteronormative teleological account of history, this display performs what decolonial scholar Walter D. Mignolo refers to as "epistemic disobedience" (2009) in its "definitive rejection of 'being told' from the epistemic privileges of the zero point what 'we' are, what our ranking is in relation to the ideal of *humanitas*[20] and what we have to do to be recognized as such" (2009:3).

Queering the Museum: possibilities and limitations

Inspired by both Darbyshire's *The Gay Museum* and Matt Smith's groundbreaking *Queering The Museum*, an exhibition held at the Birmingham

Museum and Art Gallery (UK) in 2010–2011,[21] we developed a similar project (a pop-up exhibition and symposium) in which we invited ten LGBTQ-identified Adelaidians from a variety of cultural backgrounds to each choose an object (or objects) from the History Trust of South Australia's collections, make decisions about display, and write panel text that focussed on gender and/or sexuality and/or other intersecting aspects of identity. While one of the aims of *Queering the Museum* was to explore queer histories using items from our collections, we also wanted, like Darbyshire, Smith, Wilson, and Sepahvand, to actively challenge the deeply entrenched norms, assumptions, epistemologies, and structures that underpin museum practice, and that have become so naturalised as to be almost invisible. *Queering the Museum* problematised the claim that there is an absence of LGBTIQ+ objects in our collections, and that this is true of museum collections more generally, by demonstrating that at least potentially almost all of the objects in our collections could be used to explore 'queer' (and other othered) ways of knowing and being. In doing so, the project also troubled the assumption that LGBTIQ+ objects are self-evident *as such*, and that collection catalogues capture and record the object's 'truth'.[22]

As social history museum curators we are required to document every object that comes into our collections, carefully considering its provenance and significance and using keywords to categorise it. As curatorial activists we bring to this task a critical awareness of the constructed, partial, and perspectival nature of provenance, as well as the situational character of significance – the fact that value and meaning are always determined in relation to a specific collection and collecting institution. Likewise, when we use keywords such as lesbian, gay, transgender, queer, and so on to refer to an object that was made, owned, or used by a queer-identified person, or connected to a place, event, or practice understood by the donor or curator as gay-related, we are not suggesting that the 'gayness' or 'queerness' of the object is an essential aspect of its being. Nor do we assume that objects whose catalogue entries do *not* include keywords such as these are 'not queer'. We understand these terms not as taxonomic truths but as grids of intelligibility that do not simply describe what they name, but rather constitute objects in historically and culturally specific ways. While this might seem like a fairly obvious and uncontentious claim to make, it is nevertheless at odds with the way in which museums have, historically, understood objects as things-in-themselves, and the curatorial role as the accurate and objective naming and classifying of things. This is what Bruno Latour refers to when he states that, "[f]or too long, objects have been wrongly portrayed as matters of fact" (2005:19). Drawing on the work of Latour and others we contend that if 'facts' are interpretations, then objects are necessarily open to multiple interpretations – a point we will elaborate in more detail in the following chapter.

We began the project by sharing a variety of inspiring sources with our participants including Robert Mills' desire for queer history exhibitions that

> adopt a style of presentation partly modelled on scrapbooks and collage . . . appropriate fragments, snippets of gossip, speculations, irreverent half-truths . . . resist grand narratives and categorical assertions . . . and [are] driven [not] by a desire for petrified 'history as it really was' but by the recognition that interpretations change and that our encounters with archives are saturated with desire.
>
> (2010:86–87)

We were thrilled with what emerged.[23] Barbara Baird and Vicki Rich's 'Blue Swimmers', featuring a 1950s blue wool bathing costume with the name "Mrs Stone" on a tag stitched inside, and a free-standing sign featuring the words "tour at own risk" that once adorned the quayside at Port Adelaide, offered a particularly poignant articulation of Mills' vision. The text panel that accompanied the tableaux functioned as an experimental engendering of connections rather than a statement of fact, opening with a quote from Jeanette Winterson's 'The Poetics of Sex', a playful, poetic, satirical response to heteronormative questions about lesbianism such as "Why do you sleep with girls? Which one of you is the man? What do lesbians do in bed? Were you born a lesbian? Why do you hate men? Don't you find there's something missing?"

Like Winterson whose musings continually contravene the straight and narrow, Baird and Rich refused to pin down meaning, offering instead a series of elliptical provocations, of invitations to wonder and to wander. Their text read,

> One of us had a gym teacher in high school called Mrs Stone. We got thinking about stone butches, women who sometimes passed as men, who made love to other women but did not want to be touched themselves. We can only imagine the dangerous tour of which the sign warns. We wondered about the risks that women who crossed the boundaries of sexual and gender respectability might have taken.

Placing in proximity crushes and touches, pleasures and dangers, boundaries and their contravention, Baird and Rich's contribution to *Queering the Museum* (as our pop-up exhibition, borrowing from and referencing Smith's work, was entitled), at once foregrounded the various technologies (of display, writing, speech, and so on) through which identities cohere and "take shape institutionally within museum spaces", and "[t]ransform[ed] the question 'Who is queer?' into *why* and *how* one finds queerness historically or culturally" (Mills, 2008:50).

Richard Boyle's contribution, 'Lavender Marriage' (Figure 2.4), which consisted of a mannequin dressed in a lavender wedding dress and hat made and worn during the Second World War, and a beard from a child's

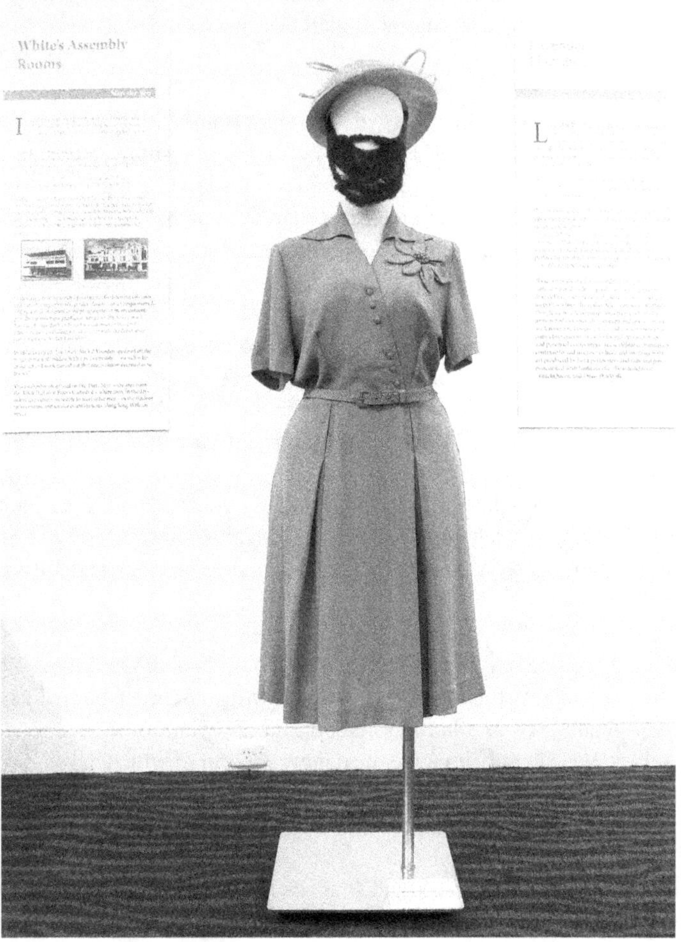

Figure 2.4 'Lavender Marriage', Richard Boyle, 2016

Credit: Courtesy of Kellie Greene

dress-up costume, functioned similarly. The mannequin was accompanied by an explanation of the thinking behind Richard's piece, and the following definitions:

> Lavender Marriage: a slang term used to describe a male female marriage-of-convenience in which one or both the partners are homosexual. Lavender Marriages were employed by . . . gays and lesbians in previous decades to conceal their sexual identity from the public.
> Beard: gay slang for a person, usually female, who is in a male female relationship primarily to conceal the other person's homosexuality.

Not only did this display introduce visitors to historical terms that they may have had no previous knowledge of, it also, in the context of fierce debate around same-sex marriage, queered both the institution of marriage and the institutionalised museological convention that assumes an indexical relation between an object and its meaning (as singular, true, and unchanging).

While *Queering the Museum* did, we like to think, function as an example of queer ethics (as outlined in the previous chapter) it also highlighted (and inevitably operated within) a range of institutional constraints. The exhibition was produced on a shoestring budget, was made possible by the generosity of participants who gave freely of their time, and ran for only two days during South Australia's annual LGBTIQ+ *Feast Festival*. Access to collections, as well as the objects available for use, was determined by a range of factors that were largely beyond our control, including time, resources, and 'appropriateness'. We were not required, as Darbyshire was by WAM, to install warning signs regarding 'adult content',[24] however, the exhibition was in a space away from the museum's main galleries and *Feast Festival* posters were displayed at the entrances, making viewers aware that the space contained LGBTIQ+ content.

Like Darbyshire, we did counter some resistance from staff who, at least initially, felt that the use of ('non queer') objects in a queer exhibition may offend those who had donated them and contributed to their catalogued interpretation. There was also some concern that opening objects up to alternative interpretations might be dangerous insofar as it could result in misinterpretation, or, worse still, some sort of anarchistic Babel, and thereby undermine the museum's credibility, its professional reputation. Rather than dismissing these concerns we saw them as providing insights into the power of museological norms, the degree to which they are deeply invested in professional selfhood, and, as such, cannot simply be dismissed at will. And rather than arguing that those who expressed them were wrong we suggested that perhaps the experiments we were undertaking in *Queering the Museum* were no more dangerous than the perception of narrow, didactic (read heteronormative) interpretations as objective, universal, ahistorical, and true (Darbyshire, 2003a:109). What impact the project will have on the way objects displayed are subsequently understood, interpreted, catalogued, and used is yet to be seen. It seems likely, however, that ultimately the hierarchy of interpretation will remain relatively unchallenged and that, at best, the displays developed by those who participated in *Queering the Museum* will be added as notes to the catalogue records for each of the items exhibited.[25] Whether this is indicative of "a reluctance to share authority, and . . . to actively promote the facilitation of conflicting points of view" (Lynch, 2011:153–154), or of the limitations of current documentation systems and structures and the costs, challenges, and potential risks involved in revising them, is difficult to say.

The art of queer/ing

Exposing institutional biases, writes Ivan Muñiz-Reed, "is not an easy task for curators, since they are working from inside the marble pillars. It has often been artists – who are better positioned to criticise the institution – working with collections, [who] have perpetrated some of the most interesting examples of epistemic disobedience" (2017:102). Similarly, Eilean Hooper-Greenhill claims that of all the strategies to challenge museums' values "some of the most revealing are those used by artists" (2000:141).

We want to end this chapter by unpicking these claims and addressing a possible objection that readers may have regarding the examples we've discussed, in particular, the fact that the majority were undertaken by artists, or in art museums, or involve the creation and/or display of artworks. Like Darbyshire, who claims that *The Gay Museum* was at once an art installation and a history exhibition, we want to queer the sort of categorical logic that subtends the all too easily assumed distinction between artist and museum practitioner, outsider and insider, artwork and science or social history display. If we acknowledge that rather than simply presenting universal, ahistorical truths in an objective and unmediated way, curators, exhibition designers, experience developers, and so on create meaning (using a whole range of mediums and techniques), then in what sense are their interventions in the world qualitatively different from those of 'artists'?

It is our contention that the differences between the roles (and the subjectivities) of museum professionals and artists is learned, institutionally regulated, an effect of particular ways of knowing and being, of situated perspectives, and as such, are open to reconfiguration, to queering. As we suggested in previous chapters, the figure of the curator as a knowledgeable, rational, objective, subject-specialist whose role is to 'translate' complex knowledge into information that is easily accessible to visitors is a construction that emerged in the nineteenth century and continues to have resonance today. Robins writes, "historically . . . museums have ameliorated impressions of partiality by assuming the unprejudiced detachment afforded to those who 'simply translate' . . . the world of material culture into classified knowledge" (2013:156). While this idea(l) (and its epistemological underpinnings) may no longer hold sway in museums to the extent that it once did, it, its attendant benefits are not as easily relinquished as we might like to imagine (as our discussion of Bourdieu's account of habitus explained).

But museum practitioners are not the only ones to have internalised idea(l)s about the museum's authoritative role in the production and dissemination of knowledge. Visitors too come armed with expectations, and while these differ depending on the individual visitor's ethos and the type of museum visited, most expect to feel confidence in the information that is offered and in its mode of delivery. In fact, the thwarting of such expectations (and the subjective investments and affective attachments associated with them) can be a source of disappointment, dis-ease, and even complaint. As a group of secondary school English teachers explained to Grant Rogers, a learning manager at the Imperial War Museum, London, they objected to the installation *Baghdad 5 March 2007* not because of the thing itself,[26] but because it was created by an artist (Jeremy Deller). They thought, explained Rogers, "that curatorial decisions should be in the hands of people who know, and people who know, are historians. That's the way it should be done because they are going to get their facts right" (cited in Robins, 2013:206). The figure of the artist, on the other hand, has a very different discursive history (or histories) as Robins (2013) demonstrates in her careful mapping of the lineage of interventionist art-practice and practitioners. Art, she suggests, has long been intimately engaged with the question of how objects, works, come to mean, and as such, those who identify with art or as artists may be more likely than, for example, curators to have developed dispositions and propensities that tend toward critique, experimentation, and disruption.[27] For the same reasons, the artist may also be more at home with the idea of their work as subjective and situated: it is, after all, much rarer to find unattributed contemporary artworks and/or interventions than it is to find anonymously authored wall panels and labels, at least in the context of museums.

Robins claims that there has been an exponential increase of late in the number of museums commissioning artists to respond to their collections (2013:1) and that this is indicative of the kind of paradigm shift that Richard Sandell called for a decade and a half ago (2003:45). This phenomenon interests us not least because it raises the question of whether and why museum staff involved in exhibition design and production are (seemingly) assumed to be constitutionally unsuited to interventionist practice. But perhaps there's more to it than that. In inviting artists to do the difficult work of institutional critique, museums put artists – rather than themselves – in the firing line: typically it is the artist who facilitates an intervention in a museum "against whom the barbs of criticism are turned. . . . [The artist] perform[s] a function on behalf of the museum and risks both being wounded and wounding, of courting the displeasure of others" (Robins, 2013:208). At the same time, the museum reaps the benefits of being positioned as progressive, supportive of diversity and inclusion, and so on, without taking responsibility for or fully committing to the content or the present and future effects of the intervention. Whilst acknowledging that these divisions are, in many senses, real, we also want to suggest that they are far from absolute. As Robins notes, "Significant others within the museum with whom the artist liaises, collaborates and coproduces are squarely implicated in any disruptions and parodic transgressions made by the artist" (Robins, 2013:213). This was very much the case with the *Queering the Museum* project we discussed earlier. From the outset we worked closely with those who produced the works, in some cases suggesting objects and theoretical readings, as well as assisting with display.[28] Robins also argues that "the most astute outcomes and strategies of artists' interventions have started to become assimilated into the repetoires of exhibition designers and curators and other museum professionals" (Robins, 2013:213), thus suggesting that museums professionals can, and indeed are, developing professional dispositions that are attuned to the queering of traditional museological roles and practices. What we hope we have demonstrated in this chapter is that there are a range of techniques that may assist museum practitioners in these endeavours. They include – but are by no means limited to – parody, irony, juxtaposition, humour, revealing without saying, foregrounding absence, parafiction, or the framing of text as artwork.[29] We might also turn for inspiration to museum tours that deploy some or all of these tactics, such as Alice Proctor's Difficult Histories tours and Victoria Fielding's An Elite Experience for Everyone.[30]

Notes

1 As Barbara Kirshenblatt-Gimblett points out, "display does not only show and speak, it does" (1998:6). In other words, display *engenders* the meanings, relations, and orientations it purports to merely present, and, through repetition, renders them 'natural' and uncontestable.

2 Harriet Tubman (1822–1913) was an abolitionist and resistance fighter who was born into slavery in Maryland. She has been widely recognised as one of the most influential Americans of the pre–Civil War period. Like Tubman, Frederick Douglass (c.1818–1895) was born into and escaped slavery in Maryland. He also became a prominent activist, author, public speaker, and leader in the abolitionist movement. Benjamin Banneker (1731–1806) was a free

African-American author, surveyor, naturalist, and farmer who was also born in Maryland to a free African-American mother and a Guinean father who was a former slave.

3 The asterisk was added in 2012 to indicate the museum's commitment to extend its focus to diverse sexualities and (non-)genders.

4 Over 30+ years the museum has staged more than 150 exhibitions and is alleged to hold the world's largest LGBTIQ+ collection.

5 For a more detailed discussion of Odarodle and its relationship to the Schwules* Museum more generally, see Liang-Kai (2018).

6 In *The Museum: Mixed Metaphors*, which took place in the African Art Gallery of the Seattle Museum in 1993, Fred Wilson inserted a western suit into a display of 'African culture' along with a label that read: "Certain elements of dress were used to designate one's rank in Africa's status-conscious capitals. A grey suit with conservatively patterned tie denotes a businessman or member of the government. Costumes such as this are designed and tailored in Africa and worn throughout the continent". This parodying of ethnographic discourse and its inversion of 'common-sense' (through the framing of what most visitors would take to be everyday clothing as 'costume') poses a similar challenge to Euro-centric, colonialist epistemologies, and the power relations they maintain, as that articulated by Saphavand.

7 As Kinsley notes, initiatives designed to recognise cultural diversity are often centred on the celebration of culturally specific holidays and annual heritage months such as African-American History Month, Women's History Month, and Cinco de Mayo. There is, she writes, "nothing wrong with celebrating events meaningful to certain communities and commemorating 'accomplishments' of traditionally minoritized groups. When these events, however, are the only time of the year certain people can 'see' themselves represented in museums. . . [it reminds us] that some groups remain subordinated in museums' day-to-day operations. . . . This type of 'one-off' initiative aimed at representing cultural diversity in museums do[es] not challenge the basic structure or canon of the museum" (2016:483–484).

8 Sepahvand mentions this at the end of 'Welcome Address'.

9 This tactic was also deployed by Sarah Brophy and Janice Hladki in *Scrapes: Unruly Embodiments in Video Art*, an exhibition held at McMaster Museum of Art, Canada, in 2010. The curators set out to "rupture embedded knowledges that otherwise tend to sediment into uninterrogated ableist and diversity discourses" (2014:316) through the creation of an unruly space filled with ambient sounds, oversized screens, bodies and objects, disruptive soundscapes, muted lighting, and pulsing colours and shapes, and also through the inclusion of works that recontextualised and nuanced the social model of disability by invoking connections to HIV/AIDS activism, indigenous land claims, and ecological abuses and activism.

10 This is in keeping with Foucault's claim that there is no outside of power, no 'innocent' vantage point from which to see and/or be. For a good introduction to the notion of power in Foucault's work, see Taylor (2011).

11 Elsewhere in *Mining the Museum* Wilson does use objects that have been intimately associated with the lives of African-American people – for example, slave manacles, a whipping post, and so on – which suggests that their absence in 'Truth Trophy' is the result of a conscious choice on behalf of the artist rather than of a lack of objects.

12 Darbyshire did not want to obscure WAM's biased history of collecting by borrowing objects to fill the exhibition. She also felt that borrowing contemporary objects would (problematically) imply that same-sex relations were a relatively new phenomenon.
13 For more detailed discussion of these techniques, see Darbyshire (2003a).
14 See Darbyshire (2003a).
15 The name came from the fact that the crab appears to be hiding its face behind its two very large pincers.
16 The text read, "One of the great disasters . . . was when we had the meeting to dissolve CAMP, which would have been about 1988, and they decided to destroy the records. I pleaded with them. . . . I said 'Put them in the Battye Library. Put a 50-year embargo on them if you want to. Don't destroy them . . . that's part of history!'. They said it would be in the spirit of the constitution (which said all the records should be kept under lock and key) to destroy them. All the minutes and all the correspondence were destroyed" (Darbyshire, 2003b:8).
17 Electroconvulsive Therapy is one of a range of pseudoscientific techniques developed in the early twentieth century to 'cure' homosexuality. It is alleged to be no longer used in most Western nations. While homosexuality is neither a crime nor considered to be a mental illness in China, in 2017 Human Rights Watch reported that private clinics and public hospitals in China continue to practise conversion therapies, including ECT. www.hrw.org/report/2017/11/15/have-you-considered-your-parents-happiness/conversion-therapy-against-lgbt-people
18 Repetition was also used in incredibly effective and affective ways in the *Exile* project at Kingston Lacy, and more specifically, In Memoriam, an installation featuring 51 knotted ropes suspended from a wooden frame and suspended in the Entrance Hall. The ropes represented the 51 men who were hanged in the UK under laws that criminalised same-sex acts during the lifetime of William Johns, who inherited the house in 1834 and who, in 1841 having been caught with a soldier in 'an indecent act', was forced into exile in France, and later, Italy. For more information, see Butler et al. (2018).
19 Such as Western Australia's Swanbourne Beach, which has operated as a beat since at least the Second World War.
20 This Latin noun meaning human nature, civilisation, and kindness was used by Cicero to describe the ideal orator and man of knowledge characteristically suited to the exercise power over others. In the *Epistulae* Pliny the Younger defined *humanitas* as the capacity to win the affections of lesser folk without impinging on the greater.
21 For a detailed account of the exhibition and the range of strategies employed, see Smith (2015) and www.youtube.com/watch?v=6ZpvLkPA5Hw.
22 For an extended critical engagement with the notion of queer objects, see Sullivan and Middleton (2019b).
23 For further discussion of the exhibition, see Sullivan and Middleton (2019a).
24 For a critique of warning signs as 'straightening devices', see Tyburczy (2016:101–124). In Sullivan and Middleton (2020) we take up Tyburczy's critique and ask why, if museums are loathe to offend visitors, signage is not used to indicate the presence of heteronormative material which would, undoubtedly, offend some visitors.
25 As part of the process of creating digital labels for display items we have recently begun exploring how to capture multiple interpretations of our collections using

the narrative module in our collection management system, KEmu (and our digital asset management system Cumulus). While pulling multiple interpretations through to digital labels is technically possible, we have not, as an institution, discussed the status of different interpretations and their relationship to one another. Another challenge is posed by the fact that only two of those who contributed to *Queering the Museum* used a single object. Each of the other exhibits involved the juxtaposition of at least two objects and this raises all sorts of questions for a documentation system that assumes an indexical relation between a single object and meaning.

26 The display consisted of the physical wreck of a car that was destroyed when a suicide bomb that killed 38 people and injured hundreds was detonated in Baghdad on 5 March 2007.

27 In making this claim we are not suggesting that it is true of all artists in all times and places.

28 From our perspective this project also queered the all-too-ready assumption of a clear distinction between insiders and outsiders. Inasmuch as we are both queer-identified and are actively involved in queer-identified circles, events, politics, we could be said to be at once inside and outside the museum. We also want to suggest, drawing on Hollows (2019), that some ‘insiders’ have more ‘outsider’ perspectives than others as a result of their particular embodied histories, their ethos. This is one reason why it is important to ensure difference and diversity within the workplace.

29 This is a strategy that Mulloway Studio used effectively in their redevelopment of the general store at the National Trust property *The Hamlet*, in Greenough, Western Australia, as a sort of ‘fake’ museum containing four fabricated objects (a sewing pattern for sandbags, conservation soap, Settler’s Own barbed wire, and a can of wheat rust) designed to provoke questions about the significance of the site and its history. The store also includes a wall covered in text (over 1,000 words) from Governor Gray’s account of an Aboriginal man walking through the country. While, on the one hand, the text might be said to be an ‘authentic’ artefact, at the same time, it constitutes a sort-of poetic intervention that raises all sorts of questions about objects, artworks, authenticity, affect, meaning-making, and so on.

30 Victoria Fielding is a character performed by Claire Robins. For further discussion see Robins (2013).

References

Ahmed, S. (2006). Orientations: Toward a Queer Phenomenology. *GLQ: A Journal of Lesbian and Gay Studies*, 12(4), 543–574.

Bennett, T. (1988). The Exhibitionary Complex. *New Formations* 4(1), 73–102.

Brophy, S., & Hladki, J. (2014). Cripping the Museum: Disability, Pedagogy, and Video Art. *Journal of Literary & Cultural Disability Studies*, 8(3), 315–333.

Butler, T., Howell, J., & Sandell, R. (2018). LGBTQ Heritage and Its Contemporary Relevance. In R. Sandell, E. Lennon, & M. Smith (Eds.), *Prejudice and Pride: LGBTQ Heritage and Its Contemporary Implications* (pp. 88–92). University of Leicester: Research Centre for Museums and Galleries (RCMG).

Castro-Gómez, S. (2005). *La Hybris Del Punto Cero: Ciencia, Raza et Ilustracion En La Nueva Granada. (1750–1816) [The Hubris of the Zero Point: Science,*

Race and Illustration in New Granada. (1750–1816)]. Bogota: Editorial Pontificia Universidad Javeriana.

Darbyshire, J. (2003a). *Restlessness of Meaning: An Exploration of How Visual Artists Are Working with Museum Collections*, unpublished Master's thesis, Curtin University of Technology.

Darbyshire, J. (2003b). *The Gay Museum: An Exhibition Exploring the History of Lesbian and Gay Presence in Western Australia*. Perth, WA: Western Australian Museum.

Fleming, M. (2010). Thinking Through Objects. In S. Lehmann-Brauns & C. Sichau Helmuth Trischler (Eds.), *The Exhibition as Product and Generator of Scholarship* (pp. 33–47). Germany: Max Plank Institute for the History of Science.

Herring, S. (2011). Material Deviance: Theorizing Queer Objecthood. *Postmodern Culture*, 21(2), retrieved March 29, 2019, from Project MUSE database.

Hollows, V. (2019). The Activist Role of Museum Staff. In R. R. Janes & R. Sandell (Eds.), *Museum Activism* (pp. 144–157). London: Routledge.

Hooper-Greenhill, E. (2000). *Museums and the Interpretation of Visual Culture*. London: Routledge.

Kinsley, R. P. (2016). Inclusion in Museums: A Matter of Social Justice. *Museum Management and Curatorship*, 31(5), 474–490.

Kirshenblatt-Gimblett, B. (1998). *Destination Culture: Tourism, Museums, and Heritage*. Berkeley: University of California Press.

Latour, B. (2005). From Realpolitik to Dingpolitik, or How to Make Things Public. In B. Latour & P. Weibel, (Eds.), *Making Things Public: Atmospheres of Democracy* (pp. 14–43). Cambridge, MA: MIT Press.

Levin, A. (2012). Unpacking Gender: Creating Complex Models for Gender Inclusivity. In E. Nightingale & R. Sandell (Eds.), *Museums, Equality and Social Justice* (pp. 156–68). London & New York: Routledge.

Liang-Kai, Y. (2018). *Performing Diverse Sexualities: Queer Curating or Curatorial Strategies of the Schwules Museum*, unpublished Master's thesis, Leiden University.

Lubar, S. (2018). Exhibiting Absence. *The Medium*, December 2. https://medium.com/@lubar/exhibiting-absence-36c5552613ba

Lynch, B. T. (2011). Collaboration, Contestation, and Creative Conflict: On the Efficacy of Museum/Community Partnerships. In J. Marstine (Ed.), *The Routledge Companion to Museum Ethics* (pp. 146–163). London: Routledge.

Mignolo, W. D. (2009). Epistemic Disobedience, Independent thought and De-Colonial Freedom. *Theory, Culture & Society*, 26(7–8), 1–23.

Mills, R. (2010). Queer Is Here? Lesbian, Gay, Bisexual and Transgender Histories and Public Culture. In A. K. Levin (Ed.), *Gender, Sexuality and Museums: A Routledge Reader* (pp. 80–88). London and New York: Routledge.

Mills, R. (2008). Theorizing the Queer Museum. *Museums & Social Issues*, 3(1), 41–52.

Moser, S. (2010). The Devil is in the Detail: Displays and the Creation of Knowledge. *Museum Anthropology*, 33(1), 22–32.

Muñiz-Reed, I. (2017). Thoughts on Curatorial Practices in the Decolonial Turn. *On Curating*, 35, 99–105.

Robins, C. (2013). *Curious Lessons in the Museum: The Pedagogic Potential of Artists' Interventions*. Farnham: Ashgate.

Sandell, R. (2007). *Museums, Prejudice and the Reframing of Difference*. London: Routledge.

Sandell, R. (2003). Social Inclusion, the Museum and the Dynamics of Sectoral Change. *Museum and Society*, 1(1), 45–62.

Sepahvand, A. (2017). *Salon Digital: Odarodle – Sittengeschichte Eines Naturmysteriums*, https://vimeo.com/241601740

Smith, M. (2015). *Making Things Perfectly Queer: Art's Use of Craft to Signify LGBT Identities*, unpublished PhD thesis, University of Brighton, UK. https://core.ac.uk/download/pdf/42558236.pdf

Smith, R. (2014). *Beyond Epistemic Disobedience: The Importance of Humour in Fred Wilson's Mining the Museum*, unpublished Master's thesis, University of British Columbia.

Sullivan, N., & Middleton, C. (2019a). Queer/ing Museological Technologies of Display. *Queer Studies in Media and Popular Culture*, 4(1), 59–70.

Sullivan, N., & Middleton, C. (2019b). Bloomers and Monocles. In C. Brickell & J. Collard (Eds.), *Queer Objects Manchester: Manchester University Press.*

Sullivan, N., & Middleton, C. (2020c). Warning! Heteronormativity: A Question of Ethics. In A. Levin & J. Adair (Eds.), *Museums, Sexuality, and Gender Activism*. London & New York: Routledge.

Taylor, D. (2011). *Michel Foucault: Key Concepts*. Durham: Acumen. Forthcoming.

Thomas, N. (2010). The Museum as Method. *Museum Anthropology*, 33(1), 6–10.

Tyburczy, J. (2016). *Sex Museums: The Politics and Performance of Display*. Chicago: University of Chicago Press.

Vogel, S. (1991). Always True to the Object, in Our Fashion. In I. Karp & S. D. Lavine (Eds.), *Exhibiting Cultures: The Poetics and Politics of Museum Display* (pp. 189–204). Washington: Smithsonian Institution Press.

Wilson, F., & Appiah, K. A. (2011). Fragments of a Conversation. In D. Globus (Ed.), *Fred Wilson: A Critical Reader* (pp. 272–302). London: Ridinghouse.

Wilson, F., & Berger, M. (2011). Collaboration, Museums, and the Politics of Display: A Conversation with Fred Wilson. In D. Globus (Ed.), *Fred Wilson: A Critical Reader* (pp. 154–168). London: Ridinghouse.

Winchester, O. (2012). A Book with Its Pages Always Open? In R. Sandell & E. Nightingale (Eds.), *Museums, Equality and Social Justice* (pp. 124–155). London: Routledge.

3 Queer/ing meaning-making

A key component of museum practice, and one that is discussed at length in almost every introductory text and on every professional body's website, is interpretation. Ideas about what interpretation is and how it might be best practised have changed over the last century or so,[1] alongside the shift from an object-focussed approach in museums to an audience-centred one: there is now less emphasis on "teachin[ing] certain truths", "revealing meanings", and "imparting understanding" (Edward P. Alexander, cited in Black, 2005:183) and more on the dialogic process of engaging audiences in meaning-making. Addressing this shift almost a quarter of a century ago Elaine Heumann Gurian stated that "In twenty five years museums will no longer be recognizable as they are now known". Museums will, she predicted, "become more comfortable with presentations that contain a multiplicity of viewpoints and with the interweaving of . . . fact and what is considered by some, but not by others, to be 'myth'" (1995:31). To what extent, then, has the future that Gurian forecast come to be?

It is now widely accepted amongst museum practitioners that visitors play an active role in interpretation and that each will interpret from their own perspective, their own ethos. There is also evidence of a growing openness to the idea that disciplinary differences between museum professionals, and/or differences between museum perspectives and those of their diverse publics, will result in multiple interpretations. However, at present the opening up of meaning to diverse interpretations is largely limited to temporary exhibitions, programmes, and projects. While the reasons for this are undoubtedly many, museum documentation lies, we suggest, at the heart of the problem. Museum documentation and, most particularly, collections management databases are "the starting point [from which] museums may define and communicate the significance and heritage value of objects" (Cameron, 2010:81)[2] and yet museum professionals rarely "apply to the register the sort of critical scrutiny to which we subject other objects in the museum" (Swinney, 2012:32). For Swinney, the term 'register' refers to both the various documentary records of collection objects – including catalogue/database entries, loan paperwork, location indexes, disposal documents, and so forth – and the process of documenting: 'register' is at once a noun and a verb, an object and a technology (a doing) (2012:32). Registers, writes Swinney "do not merely record collections, they constitute them: documentation practices are part of a technology through which collections are made and delineated" (2012:37). In other words, despite the widely held assumption that museum catalogues (and other associated forms of documentation) are largely unproblematic sources of authoritative, objective, and neutral information, they are no less an effect of processes of interpretation, selection, situated knowledges and partial vision than are the collections they archive. Far from consisting of "raw data" the document(ing) of a collection and each object therein is "but one of a multiplicity of sets of data that could have been selected to describe and delineate" (2012:34) each object and the archive that assembles them. What Swinney's analysis makes clear, then, is that museum documentation shapes (and is shaped by) what we know and what we do: it structures (and is structured by) interpretation. Given this, any attempt to open up interpretation necessarily requires us to turn a critical eye to museum documentation and the assumptions that underpin it, and, as Swinney puts it, to ask ourselves "what do we know about what we 'know' about our collections?" (Swinney, 2012:35).

The aim of this chapter is to explore the tension between the opening up of interpretation in museums and the continued hierarchisation of ways of knowing and being, between inclusion and exclusion, diversity and uniformity. In Chapter 1 we spoke at length about the ways in which inclusion discourse tends to essentialise difference, assimilate 'others' into a hetero/homonormative framework, and elide complexities. In this chapter we critically interrogate interpretation practices (most specifically labelling and cataloguing) and the epistemological assumptions that underpin them. In doing so, we queer both the belief that meaning is inherent in objects, and the pluralist/inclusive approach to 'multiple ontologies'.[3] Drawing on the work of Bruno Latour, we suggest a move away from the question of what things *mean* and towards an analysis of what things *do*, how and why. We end by asking what such a shift might mean for museum documentation, and consider some practical strategies for queering engagement with collections.

The many vs the one, or who gets to speak and why

We begin our exploration of the tensions mentioned above via a discussion of the exhibition *Lindow Man: A Bog Body Mystery*. This may seem like a strange choice for inclusion in this book since the exhibition did not focus explicitly on sexuality and/or gender, indeed, as far as we are aware, neither were mentioned although they were, of course, presumed. As Michael Warner argues, notions of sexuality and gender are inextricably bound up with

> notions of individual freedom, the state, public speech, consumption and desire, nature and culture, maturation, reproductive politics, racial and national fantasy, class identity, truth and trust, censorship, intimate life and social display, terror and violence, health care, and deep cultural norms about the bearing of the body; . . . [with] repro-narrativity: the notion that our lives are somehow made more meaningful by being embedded in a narrative of generational succession.
>
> (1991:6–7)

This exhibition could very well be said to have engaged (even if not intentionally or explicitly) with much of what Warner mentions here, in particular, with the ways in which bodies (of knowledge, flesh, the socius, or social body)[4] and the relations between them come to matter; with repro-narrativity. Our analysis will, however, focus on the no less hetero/homonormative epistemological assumptions about singularity and multiplicity, exclusion and inclusion, that subtend the positions expressed in both the aims and objectives, and criticisms, of the exhibition.

In 2008–2009, the Manchester Museum (MM) exhibited, for the third time, Lindow Man, an ancient body found in a peat bog near Manchester (UK) in 1984, and now in the collection of the British Museum. The exhibition differed significantly from previous Lindow Man exhibitions at MM, and this was due to the changes that had taken place in the museum world since the body had last been displayed there: the display of human remains was becoming an increasingly contentious issue; research carried out on and around the remains was producing disparate results, some of which challenged earlier claims about the age of the body and cause of death; there was a growing emphasis in the sector on engagement, consultation, and co-creation; and there had been an unsuccessful attempt by local activists to have the remains repatriated. Consequently the museum undertook an extensive consultation process,[5] which led to the development of an exhibition composed of textual and audio excerpts from interviews with seven people who each had a personal connection to Lindow Man: the peat diggers who discovered the remains, a local woman who had been involved in the repatriation campaign, a forensic scientist who examined the body, a Druid priest, a landscape archaeologist, and two curators, one from MM and one from the British Museum. It also included personal effects, artefacts, and specimens that contextualised these people's various connections to the body on display (Brown, 2011:130). The aim of the exhibition, as described by Pete Brown, Head of Learning and Interpretation, was to "encourage respectful self-reflection, inviting visitors to question the interpretation of archaeological evidence and the practice of displaying human remains in museums" (2011:131), and to "provoke debate" (2011:132) rather than provide a singular authoritative account of Lindow Man as previous exhibitions had.

Research that gathered and analysed feedback from staff, visitors, and volunteers, as well as media coverage and correspondence received by the museum, suggests that many people appreciated the approach taken and the provocations offered by diverse and sometimes unfamiliar perspectives (Brown, 2011). It also shows, however, that for some the exhibition was confusing, and for others, a source of anger and disdain. Rather than dismissing the criticisms received, we want instead to quote them (or references to them) at length in order to highlight some of the deeply held assumptions in which people's sense of themselves, their world, and the knowledge industries[6] with which they engage, are invested. As Brown tells it,

> some . . . staff firmly believe that the exhibition approach was perverse, flying in the face of what *we know visitors want*. For them, leaving the interpretation open is taking the lazy way out – it is a museum's job, as 'expert', to filter information and present the authorised version.
>
> (2011:132, emphasis in the original)

One staff member wrote in an email, "Public consultation is good, debate is good, but in the end the museum has a role and a duty to present *facts* as researched and integrated by *specialists*" (cited in Brown, 2011:146, emphasis added). In another email a visitor describing himself as a botanist stated that he "would prefer that museums . . . focus more on *scientific enlightenment* and *exposition* and the objects which support this process, and less on delving into the recesses of the human psyche" (cited in Sitch, 2010:378, emphasis added). Local journalist Jonathan Schofield canned the exhibition for being "wholly devoid of information", exclaiming "just give us facts please!". The museum, he wrote,

> appears to have given power of attorney to a person who has no right whatsoever to speak for the corpse. . . . [H]ow far should we allow spirituality into museums? Will it end with a priest, an imam and a 'pagan' in institutions supposedly dedicated to *reason* not superstition?
>
> (cited in Sitch, 2011:376, emphasis added)

The question of the right to speak raised by Schofield is in fact central to each of the criticisms cited here. Each implies that it is only 'the expert' who has the right, the authority, and indeed, a responsibility, to do so. Moreover, expertise is characterised not only in terms of an uncommon depth of knowledge, but also as inherently tied to rationality, objectivity, a belief in facts, and the (learned) capacity to interpret them such that they become accessible to non-experts. Much of the outrage directed at *Lindow Man: A Bog Body Mystery* was, it seems to us, an affective response to the disruption of what is perceived to be the proper order of things, an order that is, by definition, heteronormative, hierarchical, and exclusionary and that has historically been, and indeed continues to be, used to justify unequal power relations and the material effects they produce. It is perhaps unsurprising, then, that "the most vociferous criticism came . . . from more conservative members of the museum-going public" (Sitch, 2010:386), who have more to lose if heteronormative structures and the systems of power and privilege they support are queered.

In their reflections on the exhibition both Peter Brown, and the Museum's Deputy Head of Collections, Bryan Sitch, return repeatedly to the tension at the heart of the turn to pluralism and inclusion that this exhibition highlights. How, they wonder, given (some) people's habituated view of the museum as a source of sound, trusted, expert knowledge, might museums challenge exclusionary interpretation methods without alienating existing visitors and potentially undermining the institution's status and/or continued existence? Rather than answering this question we want instead to trouble it by citing four connected propositions which together open up the closed circuit created (and held in place) by the assumed either/or choice between opening up meaning and losing visitors.

The first is that the risk of alienating visitors who are challenged by exhibitions, public programmes, or interventions that critically engage with heteronormative beliefs and epistemological structures is the price museums pay for having "got their audiences accustomed to rather anodyne narratives" (Vlachou, 2018:94). Second, studies of public responses to contentious exhibitions and other forms of museum engagement suggest that the number of visitors lost as a result is often much lower than is feared. Third, when museums explicitly take a political stance, and explain to their publics what they are doing and why, they can, and do, enhance their reputation and attract new visitors (Dilenschneider, 2017). And fourth, in making decisions about practice based on *not* offending existing visitors, museums choose (although perhaps not consciously or explicitly) to continue to alienate those who are offended by heteronormative (racist, colonialist, ableist, homophobic, transphobic, classist, etc.) values and structures and the sociopolitical effects of such.[7] What this suggests is that risk-aversion can, at best, reproduce over-inflated fears that work to straitjacket change, and at worst, become a justification for not taking responsibility for the expectations museums have played a role in shaping, and for actively reconfiguring such expectations and the inequities they engender. It is worth noting here Elizabeth Wood and Sarah A. Cole's reminder that "museums are made up of individual actors" and that while decision-making power is not equally distributed in museums, each person nevertheless "needs to see that their actions can contribute to change" (2018:73) or, equally, to what Janes and Sandell refer to as "the immorality of inaction" (2018:38).

Multiple ontologies and object biographies

A decade has passed since *Lindow Man: A Bog Body Mystery* took place and it is possible, although perhaps unlikely, that, if mounted today, the same exhibition would not attract the kind of criticism it did then. We cannot be sure. Nor can we know how, or to what extent, the exhibition, and responses to it, engendered changes in museological practice at the Manchester Museum and/or elsewhere. If online catalogues are anything to go by, we can, however, suggest that this, and other similar exhibitions featuring multiple interpretations and voices, have had little impact on museum documentation practice. As Fiona Cameron claims, even the digitisation and sharing of collections online has, to date, had next to no impact on cataloguing (2008:229–230). Indeed, what we see instead is a significant gulf between the ethos of "distributed social technology practices whose strengths lie in allowing for many, contradictory perspectives" (Srinivasan, 2009:265), and the continued museological practice of privileging (to varying degrees in different areas of museum practice and different museums) singular expert accounts. This is especially troubling given that many museums are struggling with the question of relevance and trying hard, although not always with great success, to attract new publics.

Literature calling for the opening up of meaning-making in museums is diverse and motivated by a range of (sometimes conflicting) aims and objectives. As will become clear, some authors emphasise the need for a breadth of perspectives from as wide a contributor base as possible, while others are concerned with engaging very specific communities. In both cases the digital is largely understood to provide previously unimagined opportunities for engagement, and to contribute to the democratisation of museums.[8] As we will see, however, digital systems can "become analogues of their non-digital counterparts – mapping, and replicating, older representational frameworks, overwriting the capacity of the digital for radical transformation, connectivity and multiplicity with the representation of singular, teleological, narratives" (Geismar, 2018:78).

Taking a material culture studies approach to objects and their interpretation, Ramesh Srinivasan and his co-authors advocate for the collection, presentation, and documentation of "multiple ontologies" (or diverse world-views) through "in-reach programs" (Hogsden & Poulter, 2012:269) that target "expert communities who have an informed experience and interaction" (2009:269) with specific collection objects. Beginning from the premise that most collection objects in most museums have travelled from elsewhere, Srinivasan et al. argue that object biographies[9] can be "instructive of distant lives or histories" (Srinivasan, 2010:740): that they can tell us how objects were constructed, used, exchanged, collected, integrated into relations of power and privilege; how their meanings are made, changing, contingent on context, and, at times, contradictory (Curtis, 2006:122). Object biographies can also "foreground the materials that constitute an object and the historical relations that allowed those materials to come together" (Busse, 2008:194–195). However, much can be lost in the long and often complicated journey from an object's source to its place in a museum collection – not least through the imposition, upon its arrival, of discipline-specific taxonomies associated with expert knowledge – hence the call for a "vastly extended definition of expertise" (Srinivasan, 2009:267) that can include source communities. In the case of a Haida shield or Yolngu yidaki, the identification of expert communities – as those who have "a lasting, historical and informed relationship with the cultural object" (Srinivasan et al., 2009:270) – may be relatively uncontentious. However, as the objections to the Lindow Man exhibition discussed earlier suggest, extending the definition of expertise becomes much more problematic in the case of objects for which there is no easily identifiable source community. It is also difficult to imagine how it might be used to bring LGBTIQ+ perspectives into museums beyond consulting with LGBTIQ+ individuals and communities about, for example, when, where, or why a particular badge or political t-shirt might have been produced and worn.

Perhaps more concerning is the fact that whilst Srinivasan et al. call for an extended, but not entirely open-ended, definition of expertise, and thereby imply that some ways of knowing are more viable, or at least appropriate, than others, they simultaneously insist on the need to recognise, preserve, and present in an intelligible manner incommensurable ways of knowing and being without either hierarchising or unifying them. To us, this seems like a contradiction in terms: how is it possible to recognise the expertise of source communities, and, at the same time, to foster the incommensurability of multiple ontologies? Doesn't the latter aim undermine the former, not least because it ignores structural inequalities that have historically shaped different ways of knowing and being such that some have long had the status of truth, while others – most specifically those of indigenous source communities – have not and still don't? What Srinivasan et al. fail to recognise it that the "multivocal" (Phillips, 2011) model of collaboration and interpretation – which is characterised by the foregrounding of multiplicity, and not by the replacing of partial or erroneous interpretations with complete and true ones – may offer little or nothing in the way of benefits to source communities who have borne the brunt of exclusion. Even if the idea(l)s of multivocality and incommensurability may closely align with the aims and objectives of some projects (such as *Lindow Man: A Bog Body Mystery* and *Queering the Museum*), Srinivasan et al.'s vision does not provide any clues as to how entrenched notions of expertise, of who can speak and how, might be reconfigured such that multiple, perhaps even competing, interpretations and ways of knowing are given equal consideration, and historic and ongoing inequities are redressed.

There is extensive literature about the ever-increasing number of collaborations between museums and source communities that have taken place primarily in post-colonial settler nations such as Australia, Canada, and New Zealand, (Brown, 2007; Clifford, 1997; Geismar, 2018, 2012; Horwood, 2018; Peers & Brown, 2003; Rowley, 2013), and the benefits and challenges involved. Much has also been written about museum collaborations with people of colour and migrants from former colonies, designed to contribute to the decolonising of museums, the stories they tell, and the worlds they engender. What published case studies show is that there is no single model of collaboration. Rather, as Phillips argues "a spectrum of models has emerged bracketed by two distinct types" (2011:188): "multivocal" and "community-based". Phillips identifies the key characteristics of the latter as "the privileging of community ways of knowing and the identification of community members as a primary audience" (2011:195), and suggests that this form of collaboration "serves as a kind of semiotic repair kit that attaches new meanings to objects which museum visitors have become accustomed to see exclusively through the lenses of Western disciplines" (2011:195).

Even when museums set out to expose, critically engage with, and redress histories of injustice, the individuals and communities with whom they collaborate, and who have borne (and continue to bear) the brunt of systematic inequality, are often left feeling that for them the benefits have been meagre and the struggles and/or harms experienced great. Sumaya Kassim, one of the guest co-curators of *The Past is Now: Birmingham and the British Empire*, an exhibition held at Birmingham Museum and Art Gallery in 2017, explains that the experience led her to question whether mainstream museums

> can and should promote decolonial thinking or whether they are so embedded in colonial history and power structures that they will only end up co-opting decoloniality. Museums claim they want to change,

> but I'm cautious as the change often appears to be a way of managing change and radicalism, perhaps even collecting it and threading it in as part of the nation's storyline. People of colour are often the ones paying the price of decolonising. We are the ones who are rolled in to provide natural resources – our bodies, and our 'decolonial' thoughts – which are exploited and then discarded. The human cost, the emotional labour, are seen as worthy sacrifices in the name of an exhibition which can be celebrated as a successful attempt by the museum at 'inclusion' and 'decolonising', as a marker that it . . . is dealing with its past.
>
> (2017:npn)

What Kassim's experience highlights is that while projects aimed at democratising museums and including previously excluded perspectives may challenge, among other things, the singular authority of the museum, they can simultaneously expand and improve the commodity the museum trades in – that is, knowledge – and thereby contribute to its relevance, reputation, and sustainability. This may not, in itself, be a problem, however, it is if the benefits for contributing individuals and/or groups are outweighed by the costs, or are negated by outcomes that consolidate existing relations of power and privilege.[10] Sensing that this might be an inevitability, Kassim suggests that marginalised communities may "need to accept that . . . the museum will never be decolonised", and that "we don't need these places" (2017:npn).

Beliefs such as this are, perhaps, one of the many motivating factors in the establishment of non-traditional identity-based museums[11] whose remit is to collaboratively develop offerings that have at their core the perspective(s) of a particular community or peoples, and projects such as Ara Irititja and the Mukurtu Wumpurrarni-kari Archive[12] that are collaboratively developed around indigenous needs, ontologies, and protocols. There is much that can, and indeed has been, said about the political import of these institutions and projects and the various community-based approaches they employ, however, insofar as they operate outside the space of traditional museums – the structuring structures that this book sets out to queer – they are beyond the parameters of this study. Having said this, it is not our intention to dismiss these initiatives or to imply that they are less important or effective than the approaches to museum activism that we have discussed at length. As we will explain later in the chapter, rather than setting up either/or choices between different models of museum practice and/or activism, or attempting to reconcile them, we advocate instead the need for and importance of multiple approaches strategically deployed to address particular situations and issues and achieve specific outcomes.

Networked collections and the transformation of knowledge

Taking a very different approach to challenging heteronormative museological interpretation practices and the assumptions that underpin them, Fiona Cameron turns her attention to the digitisation and sharing of collections online and the unprecedented opportunity she claims this provides for rethinking collections, their interpretation, and documentation. Collection objects and information, she writes "now operates within networks[13] that transcend their immediate location, placing them in wider flows of interconnected cultural, political, economic, and technological ideas, agendas, and resources" (2008:230). This conception of objects and their interpretation as networked suggests that objects are never simply things-in-themselves, or, to use a phrase from Bruno Latour (2004), "matters of fact". In making this claim we are not suggesting that facts are fallacious and should therefore be rejected:[14] to do so would be to posit a fact about the non-existence of facts! It is perhaps worth clarifying here, then, that as we understand it poststructuralism, and, by association, queer theory, "is not a dogma that demands that we all reject 'facts'. . . . The point . . . of poststructuralism isn't to say that 'anything goes', it is to explore and analyse how 'truths' are mobilized and meted out" (Crilley & Chatterje-Doody, 2018:2), how some ways of knowing, doing, and being are legitimised, normalised, and take on the mantle of 'common sense', while others are marginalised, delegitimised, and silenced. In short, the central concern of poststructuralism, and thus queer praxis, is relations of power and the role that knowledge plays in their maintenance and/or resistance.[15]

For Latour and those who subscribe to the network model, objects acquire their meaning and significance from a large number of elements: "from curatorial disciplines, their production and consumption contexts, their practical use in everyday life and within networks as technical, social and political entities" (Cameron, 2008:238), from their sedimented histories, "the buildings in which they reside, the images that represent them, and the texts which are written about them" (Byrne et al., 2011:10). Objects, writes Latour, are "more interesting, variegated, uncertain, complicated, far reaching, heterogeneous, risky, historical, local, material and networky" (2005:11) than we most often presume. What matters to those who advocate a network approach is not so much what objects *mean*, but rather, what they *do*: for Latour, objects are "active agents in the formation of people, institutions, cultures" (Cameron & Mengler, 2009:211), and it is their capacity to *assemble* that matters.

Consider for a moment how human remains and their display (both historically and in the present) have generated different connections, emotions, opinions, and dis/agreements; invited legal, spiritual, historical, ethical, scientific, and diverse political and cultural perspectives; and gathered together a wide range of people, each with their own embodied histories, dispositions, and agendas. Or, likewise, how same-sex marriage, sex education in schools, and memorials to 'great white men',[16] have all engendered a whole range of issues, debates, positions, and emotions, that suggest that their meaning is far from innate, singular, universal, or fixed. Of course, the potential of objects to do this will be determined, at least in part, by where and how they are (re)presented: buried amongst myriad other objects in a massive online collection they are probably unlikely to attract much attention, but framed somehow, as objects are in exhibitions, public programmes, and/or projects (that is, in connection with a particular issue, or in relation to other objects), they may well assemble networks of people, ideas, and things, particularly if they are accessible beyond the walls of the museum.

If, as this model suggests, objects and the meanings and values attributed to them are effects of complex networks, we might conclude that the singular interpretation of objects in museums is achieved through decontextualisation – the removal or severing of objects from particular networks – and recontextualisation – the imposition of historical, cultural, and discipline-specific frames of reference or networked connections. These processes not only shape the meaning and relationships of the objects museums collect, they also remove complexities, render objects, their meanings, and relationships static, and thereby contain and constrain their (queer) potentiality. Objects thus become what Latour (1987) refers to as "immutable mobiles", shackled to fixed taxonomies and the epistemologies that subtend them. At the same time, these generative processes are covered over by the notion of significance articulated as it is in collections documentation as definitive and unchanging (except perhaps in cases where it is found to be erroneous). A network approach seeks to (re)activate the potential force of objects to assemble and transform people and ideas, to open up space for debate and for new knowledges and practices to emerge. Hence for Latour, the role of the critic is not to debunk but to assemble, not to "lift the rugs from under the feet of the naive believers" but, rather, to offer "participant arenas in which to gather" (2004:246).

It is important to clarify here that what drives this approach is a commitment to complexity and transdisciplinarity rather than plurality and inclusion. As we have suggested throughout this book, inclusion discourse with its emphasis on the value of diversity or plurality is underpinned by, and reaffirms, the idea(l) of unity as a social good. However, unless we are all clones with the exact same histories, corporealities, (dis)positions, privileges, and so on, there can be no social good into which we all slot comfortably: what is good for one will necessarily *not* be good for another and consequently inclusion will always, and cannot but, engender exclusion. Complexity, on the other hand, is less an ideal or political goal than a critical tool that gestures towards, and may be helpful in exploring, the dense entanglements in which people and things, ideas and feelings, actions and relations come to matter. Similarly, the notion of transdisciplinarity can help us to understand the disciplinary frames that shape things in specific ways and hold them in place and, at the same time, provide ways of thinking beyond them, of queering them and the effects they produce.

While the network model sounds compelling in theory, its practical application may prove challenging. For example, open invitations to online users to provide feedback on, or contribute information to, online catalogues are rarely taken up with abandon.[17] At the same time, there is a fear amongst (some) museum professionals that open calls for user-generated content may[18] result in an unmanageable amount of information and/or in contributions that are not deemed of sufficient quality to be of use. They may also, warn Hogsden and Poulter, "distance special-interest users from offering their insights to inform museum collections" (2012:275), in particular if it is thought that the information that they contribute will be accorded equal (or lesser) status than information provided by 'others', such as interpretations that challenge or perhaps negate their own.

Notes on practice

Museum cataloguing systems tend to be rather blunt objects that do not easily lend themselves to the recording of multiple ontologies, networked matters of concern, or meaning-making practices that are other than textual. This is not to suggest that such systems are not open to more innovative usage or that they are not constantly being adapted to better fit the changing needs of the sector. Our point here is that the development of new ways to engage with cataloguing systems is unlikely to happen in workplaces where resources are already stretched, unless they are prioritised and integrated into strategic plans focussing specifically on reconfiguring traditional museological practice and its underlying epistemological structure, its articulation in *all* areas of practice, and the social, political, and economic effects of such.

It is imperative, argues Cameron, and we agree, that we "revisit the . . . epistemological foundations on which documentation is formulated" (Cameron, 2010:83) and "put the complexity back into collections records in ways that resonate with complex and multi-dimensional lived realities to which collections now connect" (Cameron & Mengler, 2009:193). So how might we begin to develop new knowledge environments that attempt to articulate rather than disavow complexity? What might it mean for museums to make a real commitment to situate knowledges, to foreground partial vision, to bear witness to difference, to acknowledge and redress histories of injustice? And how, given the widely held view of museums as sources of reliable information, might we achieve these things and simultaneously maintain the museum's credibility, and avoid overly confusing or alienating visitors? Moreover, what might all this mean with regard to "the register"?

Exposing interpretive frameworks (rather than assuming that collections information is neutral) is a good place to start to queer/ing documentation. We can, for example, make transparent the fact that the interpretation given and the significance accorded an object are contextually specific by explicitly addressing the policy and/or thinking that led to its being collected. We can document the circumstances under which it was collected (was it actively sought, and if so, why); who interpreted its meaning and significance, using what criteria and why; where and when the interpretation took place, and why this matters; whether there are competing interpretations that the person cataloguing is aware of (Cameron, 2010:85). This is not a case of recording information for purely administrative purposes, but rather of acknowledging that these processes are situated and subjective, and that they construct knowledge, shape objects and their relations, and contribute to world-making: that they are, and cannot not be, political.[19] Catalogue records, writes Cameron, are "an 'artefact' of [the] time, place, and social context" (2010:87) in which they were created, and of the individual who authored them. As such, they are never definitive, but should be considered instead as always in process. Consequently, Cameron suggests that "we need to instill a reflexive consciousness among curators regarding the limited legitimacy and lifespan of collections information", and that a "program of collections information revision and archiving needs to be instituted as part of the documentation process" (2010:87). Practically, this may be a resource-heavy strategy that is difficult to implement, but it is, we contend, nevertheless worth considering.

Documentation might also expose, rather than veiling over, the epistemological or disciplinary frameworks that shape particular interpretations of an object and its significance. As Hooper-Greenhill notes in *Museums and the Shaping of Knowledge*, "the same material object entering the disciplines of different ensembles of practice, would be differently classified" (1992:7). Thus a silver teaspoon could be interpreted as an object that is indicative of an industry that is specific to a given time and place, or as something that enables us to talk about a particular technological innovation, or as a piece of decorative art that fits in a chronological stylistic framework, or as an object that has personal significance for its owner. The specificity of these interpretations could be made apparent by linking significance statements to the institution's collecting policy, and by being explicit about the fact that the object may be interpreted entirely differently in a context that employs a different disciplinary frame and thereby locates the object in different networks.

As well as exposing interpretive frameworks, museum practitioners might also employ a range of strategies designed to acknowledge and make visible multiplicity, open-endedness, relationality. For example, catalogue entries could provide links to related sources such as exhibition websites, scholarly works, bibliographies, information about materials and manufacturing, and about geopolitical issues and relations associated with production, regulation, distribution and consumption, newspaper stories, auction catalogues, diaries and letters, and other collection records in order to provide a much fuller picture of the contexts that shape objects, their uses, and their (ongoing) interpretations. As Cameron points out, "research files, documents, recorded interviews, graphics, audio/visuals, publications, interactives and educational materials are all currently held in separate files and collections" (2010:90). Making these components accessible and easily navigable through flexible multi-media, user-driven, delivery systems would enhance user-generated interpretation, and, along with provision for input of user-generated interpretation, would expand not only what we know, but also how we know. It would also clearly demonstrate that objects "are involved in complex web[s] of agency, as they produce and are produced by their interactions with other agents and the world" (Byrne et al., 2011:6).[20]

As we've already discussed, sourcing interpretations, taxonomies, and forms of engaging with objects from individuals and communities outside the museum, and including these in collections documentation would also expand current meaning-making systems and redress the historical marginalisation of some knowledges, practices, identities, and the privileging of others. Similarly, collaborations with museum professionals from different disciplinary backgrounds may enable the authoring of multi- or trans-disciplinary statements of meaning and significance. Moving away from a primarily text-based model of documentation also opens up space for multiple ontologies: audio visual technologies, for example, may enable the documentation of multiple interpretations of, interactions with, and connections between objects that are difficult to capture through words alone. And as we will see in the following chapter, the 3D rendering of objects, and their translation into light, sound, and other communicative and/or affective mediums, can radically challenge heteronormative forms of object engagement and documentation.

None of these strategies are new, but nor are they easily implemented. Indeed, they highlight, as Cameron suggests, "the tension between the potential richness collections have to offer and museums as relatively poorly resourced cultural institutions" (2010:91). At the same time, they challenge deeply held (and often unconscious) investments in order, continuity, linearity, determinacy, predictability, universality, orthodoxy, authority and expertise, and thus they trouble our (professional) identities[21] – our very being-in-the-world (of museums).

Notes

1 According to many commentators, interpretation, as understood in a museological context, began with the work of American naturalist and National Parks guide, Enos Mills (1870–1932), and was popularised with the publication of Freeman Tilden's landmark book *Interpreting Our Heritage* in 1957. Tilden defined interpretation as "an educational activity which aims to reveal meanings and relationships through the use of original objects, by firsthand experience, and by illustrative media" (1957:9).
2 Cameron cites Gaynor Kavanagh (1990) who argues that it is at the level of individual object records that heteronormative practices take root (cited in Cameron, 2010:81).
3 This term is used to refer to refer to differing (and often competing) understandings of the nature of being.
4 Sometimes referred to as the 'body politic'.
5 For more information see Sitch (2010:372–376).
6 For more on knowledge industries, and, more particularly, the need to queer them, see our K.I.N.Q. Manifesto, Sullivan and Middleton (2018).
7 For more in-depth engagement with this claim, see Sullivan and Middleton (2019) and Sentance (2018)
8 Online participation as a means by which to democratise museums and other GLAM sector organisations has taken numerous forms including tagging, objectwikis, folksonomies, and crowd curation.
9 The notion of 'object biographies' is derived primarily from the work of Appadurai (1986) and Kopytoff (1986).
10 Sumaya Kassim states "Put simply, to decolonise is to remember. It is to say 'we have met before; that, we are here because you were there'. And it is to recalibrate how we interact with each other with that earlier meeting in mind". For her, the recalibration that is essential to decolonisation did not happen in her collaboration with BMAG.
11 For example, the Museum of Romani Culture in Brno, Czech Republic; the Sarakatsani Folklore Museum in Serres, Greece; the Museum of the American Indian in New York, USA; the Japanese American National Museum in Los Angeles, USA; the Haida Heritage Centre in Skidegate, British Columbia, Canada; the Jewish Museum of Australia in Victoria; the GLBT History Museum in San Francisco, USA; the Leather Archives and Museum in Chicago, USA; the Bonn Women's Museum, Germany; and the online Disability History Museum.
12 For more information, see Ridgeway (2017).
13 From the perspective taken by Cameron, Latour, and others drawing on and contributing to what has become known as Actor Network Theory (ANT), a network is less a thing, than a framework for understanding flows, relationality, and becomings (as opposed to being).
14 Indeed, Latour is troubled by the perceived proximity between poststructuralist critiques of truth, and the 'post-truth' ethos that have led writers such as Calcutt

(2016) and Scruton (2017) to characterise poststructuralism as the evil progenitor of post-truth politics. For more on this claim and criticisms of it, see Edsall (2018).

15 For Foucault (1980) power and knowledge are inextricably related: knowledge is always an exercise of power and power is always a function of knowledge.

16 We use the term 'object' here to refer not only to tangible, material things that can be seen, touched, and so on, but also to practices, relationships, "objects of thought, feeling, and judgement, as well as objects in the sense of aims, aspirations, and objectives" (Ahmed, 2006:56).

17 This may be less of an issue in cases of focussed, purposive projects whose aims, objectives, and parameters are clearly defined such as the British Museum's Talking Objects programme. For a detailed analysis of this programme, see Hogsden and Poulter (2012).

18 This is a fear that has not as yet been realised and may in fact never be. It is nevertheless worth attending to since it forces us to reflect on what we assume radical openness might entail, what it might achieve, and how.

19 This approach challenges the empiricist tradition in which documentation is understood as "the collation of self-evident data [or facts] derived from the object as source" of meaning (Cameron, 2010:83). It thus questions the tendency in heteronormative documentation to emphasise physical description and other 'verifiable' details such as size, date, maker, and so on (Cameron, 2010:84).

20 *Unpacking the Collection* provides case studies that illustrate the multiple kinds of agents and agency that contribute to and shape museum collections and the objects therein. In the introduction to the collection Sarah Byrne, Anne Clarke, Rodney Harrison, and Robin Torrence provide a useful diagram outlining these nodes within networks. They include the following: Creator Community (production, use/display, gifting/selling, withholding/hiding); Field Agent/Collector (collecting, stealing/taking, selecting/disposing, classifying, recording, storing, publishing, exhibiting, gifting/selling/exchanging); Collector/Broker/Auction House (selecting/disposing/selling/exchanging, classifying, recording, storing, publishing, exhibiting, gifting); Museum/Curator (selecting/disposing, classifying, recording, storing, publishing, exhibiting, re-engaging with creator communities, repatriating, acquiring things and knowledges); Public (visiting/not visiting, viewing, learning, passing on knowledge/contesting, circulating references/images) (2011:7).

21 Here we refer to both the understanding we have of ourselves (which, as we explained earlier in the book, is shaped by the habitus in which we come to be professionals), and the conception and associated expectations that others have of us.

References

Ahmed, S. (2006). *Queer Phenomenology: Orientations, Objects, Others*. Durham: Duke University Press.

Appadurai, A. (1986). *The Social Life of Things: Commodities in Cultural Perspective*. Cambridge: Cambridge University Press.

Black, G. (2005). *The Engaging Museum: Developing Museums for Visitor Involvement*. London: Routledge.

Brown, D. (2007). Te Ahu Hiko: Digital Cultural Heritage and Indigenous Objects, People and Environments. In F. Cameron & S. Kenderdine (Eds.), *Theorizing*

Digital Cultural Heritage: A Critical Discourse (pp. 77–93). Cambridge, MA: MIT Press.

Brown, P. (2011). Us and Them: Who Benefits from Experimental Exhibition Making? *Museum Management and Curatorship*, 26(2), 129–148.

Busse, M. (2008). Museums and the Things in Them Should Be Alive. *International Journal of Cultural Property*, 15(2), 189–200.

Byrne, S., Clarke, A., Harrison, R., & Torrence, R. (2011). Networks, Agents, and Objects: Frameworks for Unpacking Museum Collections. In S. Byrne et al (Eds.), *Unpacking the Collection: Networks of Material and Social Agency in the Museum* (pp. 3–26). New York: Springer.

Calcutt, A. (2016). The Surprising Origins of 'post-truth' – and How it Was Spawned by the Liberal Left. *The Conversation*, November 18. https://theconversation.com/the-surprising-origins-of-post-truth-and-how-it-was-spawned-by-the-liberal-left-68929

Cameron, F. (2010). Museum Collections, Documentation, and Shifting Knowledge Paradigms. In R. Parry (Ed.), *Museums in the Digital Age* (pp. 80–95). London: Routledge.

Cameron, F., & Mengler, S. (2009). Complexity, Transdisciplinarity, and Museum Collections Documentation. *Journal of Material Culture,* 14(2), 189–218.

Cameron, F. (2008). Object-oriented Democracies: conceptualising museum collections in networks. *Museum Management and Curatorship*, 23(3), 229–243.

Clifford, J. (1997). *Routes: travel and translation in the late twentieth century*. Cambridge: Harvard University Press.

Crilley, R., & Chatterje-Doody, P. (2018). Security Studies in the Age of 'Post-Truth' Politics: In Defence of Poststructuralism. *Critical Studies on Security*, 1–5. DOI: 10.1080/21624887.2018.1441634.

Curtis, N. (2006). Universal Museums, Museum Objects, and Repatriation: The Tangled Lives of Things. *Museum Management and Curatorship*, 21(2), 117–227.

Dilenschneider, C. (2017). MoMA Sees Reputation Boost After Displaying Muslim Artists. *Know Your Own Bone*, March 8. www.colleendilen.com/2017/03/08/moma-sees-reputation-boost-after-displaying-muslim-artists-data/

Edsall, T. (2018). Is President Trump a Stealth Postmodernist of Just a Liar? *New York Times*, January 12. www.nytimes.com/2018/01/25/opinion/trump-postmodernism-lies.html

Foucault, M. (1980). *Power/Knowledge: Selected Interviews & Other Writings 1972–1977*, C. Gordon, L. Marshall, J. Mepham, & K. Soper (Trans.). New York: Pantheon Books.

Geismar, H. (2018). *Museum Object Lessons for the Digital Age*. London: UCL Press.

Geismar, H. (2012). Museum + Digital? In H. A. Horst & D. Miller (Eds.), *Digital Anthropology* (pp. 166–187). London: Berg.

Gurian, E. H. (1995). A Blurring of the Boundaries. *Curator: The Museum Journal*, 38(1), 31–37.

Hogsden, C., & Poulter, E. (2012). The Real Other? Museum Objects in Digital Contact Networks. *Journal of Material Culture*, 17(3), 265–286.

Janes, R. R., & Sandell, R. (2018). Posterity Has Arrived: The Necessary Emergence of Museum Activism. In R. R. Janes & R. Sandell (Eds.), *Museum Activism* (pp. 35–53). London: Routledge.

Kassim, S. (2017). The Museum Will Not Be Decolonised. *Media Diversified*. https://mediadiversified.org/2017/11/15/the-museum-will-not-be-decolonised. Accessed March 10, 2019.

Kavanagh, G. (1990). *History Curatorship*. Leicester and London: Leicester University Press.

Kirshenblatt-Gimblett, B. (1992). Objects of Ethnography. In B. Kirshenblatt-Gimblett (Ed.), *Destination Culture: Tourism, Museums and Heritage* (pp. 17–79). Berkeley: University of California Press.

Kopytoff, I. (1986). The Cultural Biography of Things. In A. Appadurai (Ed.), *The Social Life of Things: Commodities in Cultural Perspective* (pp. 64–91). Cambridge: Cambridge University Press.

Latour, B. (2005). From Realpolitik to Dingpolitik, or How to Make Things Public. In B. Latour & P. Weibel (Eds.), *Making Things Public: Atmospheres of Democracy* (pp. 14–43). Cambridge, MA: MIT Press.

Latour, B. (2004). Why Has Critique Run Out of Steam? From Matters of Fact to Matters of Concern. *Critical Inquiry*, 30(2), 225–248.

Latour, B. (1987). *Science in Action: How to Follow Scientists and Engineers Through Society*. Cambridge, MA: Harvard University Press.

Munro, E. (2014). Doing Emotion Work in Museums: Reconceptualising the role of community engagement practitioners. *Museum & Society*, 12(1), 44–60.

Peers, L., & Brown, A. K. (2003). *Museums and Source Communities: A Routledge Reader*. London: Routledge.

Phillips, R. B. (2011). Toward a Dialogic Paradigm: New Models of Collaborative Curatorial Practice. In R. B. Phillips (Ed.), *Toward the Indigenization of Canadian Museums* (pp. 185–204). McGill: McGill Queen's University Press.

Ridgeway, B. (2017). This Sense of Place/This Living Archive: Cocreative Digitization and First Nations People's Remembering. *Collections: A Journal for Museums and Archives Professionals*, 13(2), 185–198.

Rowley, S. (2013). The Reciprocal Research Network: The Development Process. *Museum Anthropology Review*, 7(1–2), 22–43.

Scruton, R. (2017). Post-Truth? It's Pure Nonsense. *The Spectator*, June 10. www.spectator.co.uk/2017/06/post-truth-its-pure-nonsense/

Sentance, N. (2018). Engaging with the Uncomfortable. *Archival Decolonist [-o-]*, April 8. www.archivaldecolonist.com

Sitch, B. (2010). Consultation or Confrontation? Lindow Man: A Bog Body Mystery. In *The New Museum Community: Audiences, Challenges, Benefits* (pp. 366–393). London: MuseumsEtc.

Srinivasan, R., Becvar, K. M., Boast, R., & Enote, J. (2010). Diverse Knowledges and Contact Zones with the Digital Museum. *Science, Technology & Human Values*, 35(5), 735–768.

Srinivasan, R., Boast, R, Furner, J., & Becvar, K. M. (2009). Digital Museums and Diverse Cultural Knowledges: Moving Past the Traditional Catalogue. *The Information Society*, 25(4), 265–278.

Sullivan, N., & Middleton, C. (2019). Warning! Heteronormativity: A Question of Ethics. In A. Levin & J. Adair (Eds.), *Museums, Sexuality, and Gender Activism*. New York: Routledge.

Sullivan, N., & Middleton, C. (2018). The KINQ Manifesto. In T. Jones (Ed.), *Bent Street 2: Australian LGBTIQA+ Arts, Writing & Ideas*. Melbourne: Clouds of Magellan.

Swinney, G. (2012). What Do We Know About What We Know? The Museum "register" as Museum Object. In S. Dudley, A. J. Barners, J. Binnie, J. Petrou, & J. Walklate (Eds.), *The Thing About Museums: Objects and Experience, Representation and Contestation* (pp. 31–46). London and New York: Routledge.

Tilden, F. (1957). *Interpreting Our Heritage: Principles and Practices for Visitor Services in Parks, Museums, and Historic Places*. Minneapolis: University of Minnesota.

Vlachou, M. (2018). Dividing Issues and Mission-Driven Activism. In R. R. Janes & R. Sandell (Eds.), *Museum Activism* (pp. 87–100). London: Routledge.

Warner, M. (1991). Introduction: Fear of A Queer Planet. *Social Text*, 29, 3–17.

Wood, E., & Cole, S. A. (2018). Growing an Activist Museum Professional. In R. R. Janes & R. Sandell (Eds.), *Museum Activism* (pp. 72–86). London: Routledge.

4 Queer/ing engagement

Community engagement is regularly posited as a means by which museums can invite individuals and groups who do not regularly visit to contribute to the institution and to help shape its aims, objectives, foci, and practice, and thereby achieve a sense of investment and belonging (Perkin, 2010:108).[1] As such, community engagement is largely understood as one of the key areas of museum practice that "contribut[es] to social policy objectives around social inclusion" (Munro, 2014:48). But as Nuala Morse argues, community engagement has also emerged in response to non-governmental demands from outside the sector (Morse, 2018:172; Perkin, 2010:108)[2] for minority representation around issues of race, gender, sexuality, dis/ability, and so on (2018:172). And as we noted in the previous chapter, community engagement has come to be understood by some as a political commitment to the recognition and sharing of multiple ontologies through the co-creation of exhibitions, programmes, and projects that foreground diverse ways of knowing, being, and doing (Morse, 2018:172). Cornwall and Gaventa encapsulate these tendencies in the claim that over the last couple of decades there has been a shift in the museological conception of communities from "users and choosers to makers and shapers" (cited in Lynch, 2011, 441).

Even a very cursory survey of available literature shows that in practice community engagement is a beast with many faces, that it is as diverse as the groups it is intended to serve.[3] As such, it produces a range of outcomes and socio-political effects: "from placation and potential exploitation to so called 'empowerment' of communities" (Onciul, 2015:92). In other words, far from simply achieving the aim(s) of inclusion, community engagement can, and, as Sumaya Kassim's experience discussed in the previous chapter shows, sometimes does, result in the reproduction of inequalities, exploitation, and exclusion. Given this, we take seriously Bernadette Lynch's claim that museums need to "get past their assumptions and rhetoric" (2011:443), and gain "sufficient critical distance to analyse their work in this area"

(2011:444). The most obvious place to begin the work of critical interrogation is with the notion of community.

Community and its discontents

While the notion of community is ubiquitous in museum discourse, its use is largely "uncritical and undefined" (Pishief, 2017:83): given this, it needs "to be approached with some caution" (Crooke, 2006:177). In keeping with the account of ethics offered in Chapter 1, Joseph describes "the practice of critique, and in particular a critical relationship to community, as an ethical practice of community" (cited in Strickland, 2004:182). In this chapter we offer an enactment of ethics that queers commonly held understandings of community, the assumptions about identity, social relations, and political practice that inform them, and the problems or discontents that have arisen as a result. We do this, first, by critically analysing the notion of community, and second via a consideration of the ways in which this notion (and its attendant epistemological assumptions) operates in three different examples of collaborative practice.

The *Oxford Living Dictionaries* defines community as "a group of people living in the same place or having a particular characteristic in common; a group of people living together and practising common ownership; a body of nations or states unified by common interests; the condition of sharing or having certain attitudes and interests in common" (npn). What characterises community, according to the definitions offered here, then, is commonality: a common identity, a common purpose, a shared ethos (ways of knowing, being, and doing that are integral to identity) that unifies individuals and differences. The implication is that those who share an identity will have ways of knowing, being, and doing in common, and vice versa. This is precisely how Nina Simon characterises community in *The Art of Relevance*. Community, she writes, refers to "a group of people who share something in common. . . . You can define a community by the shared attributes of the people in it and/or by the strength of the connections among them. You need a bunch of people who are alike in some way, who feel some sense of belonging or interpersonal connection" (2016:87). It is our contention that despite (or perhaps even because of) its persuasive, common-sense character, this idea(l) of community is, nevertheless, deeply problematic.

In her critique of lesbian identity and politics, Shane Phelan (1994) identifies two models of community that embrace this idea(l) of unity through commonality: these are the ascriptive and the nonascriptive models. The ascriptive model, which subtends most museum-driven engagements with groups identified as appropriate partners for specific collaborative projects, is founded on the assumption of a 'natural' basis for community. Race, for example, can be, and often is, seen as a natural basis for community, and the same is true of gender or sexuality (if defined as biologically determined). We might speak, for example, of the lesbian community and imply that all lesbians share a fundamental commonality, and that this naturally takes precedence over differences in location, race, nationality, class, gender, ethnicity, spirituality, age, ability, occupation, political disposition, and so on. On this model, the core identity of the individual precedes the community that naturally and inevitably forms around it. But as we know only too well, assumed biological commonalities are no guarantee of unity. Debates within feminism(s), for example, have long shown that differences between, amongst, and within women are not simply surmountable by claiming that, at a fundamental level, women share a common biological essence. In fact, rather than resulting in a unified and coherent community, this assumption functions to exclude multiplicity by ignoring the complex, intersecting, lived realities of those who identify as women, and in doing so causes all sort of rifts and divisions within so-called feminist communities.[4]

Alternatively, community can be conceived as a voluntary alliance of individuals formed in order to create and maintain particular identities and lifestyles. Leather and/or SM communities could be seen as examples of nonascriptive communities if we understand sexual practice and/or identity as other than innate.[5] This model of community may appear to be antithetical to the ascriptive model insofar as the focus on conscious choice implies that identity is an effect of identification rather than an innate essence. However, Phelan argues that the seeming opposition between "natural communities" (ascriptive model) and "created communities" (nonascriptive model) is not as clear-cut as it may first appear, and that while the nonascriptive model of community does not conceive identity as essential it nevertheless tends to circumscribe it. This is apparent in the case of *Lindow Man: A Bog Body Mystery*, and the question it provoked of who could or should speak about the remains, why, and how. The criticisms made by both museum practitioners and those outside the profession were all informed by, and reproduced, a nonascriptive understanding of community – in this case, the community of experts. While this community was not assumed to be biologically determined, in the minds of the exhibition's critics it was nevertheless imagined as clearly bounded. Consequently, much of the dis-ease expressed stemmed from the fear that the boundary that divides experts from non-experts was undermined by the approach taken.[6]

What we see here is that the nonascriptive model of community, like the ascriptive model, is subtended by what Iris Marion Young refers to as "the logic of identity" (1986:3). Put simply, both models presume that identity is a matter of fact regardless of whether or not it is natural or cultural: both imply that I can designate myself as, for example, a leather daddy, a muslim, a Deaf woman, a Wiradjeri man, and that this identity is self-evident, singular, mutually exclusive, unambiguous, uncontentious, and the source of commonality with some and difference from others. But we know from experience that identity is rarely, if ever, this simple a matter. The same can be said of community. "The notion of a singular, unified lesbian community is absurd", writes Lisa Chang Hall.

> Even if every lesbian in the United States was white, middle-class, able-bodied, Christian-raised, and living in the urban environment, there would still be bar dykes, sports dykes, women who aren't into roles, radical politicos, butches, separatists, s/m leather girls, those who aren't lesbians but who are just in love with 'x', believers in the Lesbian Nation, femme tops, Young Republicans, assimilationists, . . . piercing queens, . . . and that's just for starters.
>
> (Chang Hall, 1993:225)[7]

More troubling still is the fact that if the unified identity of the community (and/or the individual) is to remain intact then the borders between self and other, inside and outside, us and them, must, as the criticisms aimed at *Lindow Man* clearly demonstrated, be firmly drawn and maintained (1986:3). In other words, community, as it is conventionally understood necessarily entails the exclusion of those who do not and cannot belong, and the continual patrolling of the boundaries between those who do and those who do not. Consequently, debates regarding who should be allowed membership of a particular community, access to community events and spaces, the right to speak, and on what basis such judgements could and should be made, are rife within and amongst communities regardless of whether the source of their presumed commonality is understood as essential or self-nominated. It is little wonder then that community engagement, which is so often fraught and far from simply engendering inclusion, can involve the fracturing of communities (both those inside the museum and those who are collaborating with the museum) and/or the further entrenching of presumed distinctions between groups.

So, what do we do about 'community'? Before we elaborate alternative ways of thinking about community engagement and the conception of community that informs it, we want to make it clear that in offering the earlier critique our intention is not to suggest that the notion of community as a matter of fact is erroneous or wholly misguided and should therefore be abandoned. We are mindful that in some contexts adopting an essentialist position with respect to identity categories can be a powerful way to mobilise resistance to dominant structures and the systems of power and privilege they support. Essentialism, writes Gayatri Chakravorty Spivak, "is like dynamite, or a powerful drug: judiciously applied, it can be effective in dismantling unwanted structures or alleviating suffering" (cited in Duncanson, 2005:28). However, as she goes on to warn, when uncritically employed, essentialism is destructive and addictive. Indeed, the fact that it has long been employed by those in positions of power to fix the identities and the inferior status of others – women, non-white, and indigenous others, queers, the poor, those whose anatomies or psyches are atypical, and so on – and the superior status of white, able-bodied, cisgendered, heterosexual, men should in itself urge caution.

It is the double-edged character of essentialism that led Spivak to posit the notion of "strategic essentialism" as a political tactic that minority groups can make an informed choice to take up in order to redress structural inequalities and past abuses.[8] This might play out in a museum setting in a variety of ways. For example, a diverse group of people identifying as gay men might knowingly choose to foreground their same-sex attraction over other aspects of their identity, and over the differences between them, in an exhibition or public programme designed to challenge heteronormative assumptions about parenthood. Similarly, a group of Indigenous Australians from a diverse range of nations might choose to foreground their identity as First Nations peoples in order to challenge settler-colonialism and claim sovereignty of the lands that were taken from them and never ceded.

At the same time, "recognizing the risks of building communities on essential [or non-essential but nevertheless delimiting] notions of identity, universal assumptions, or them-and-us binaries" (Baker & Scheele, 2016:169) may mean that we strategically choose to take a different path. Bryony Onciul offers one option when she replaces the definition of communities as "homogenous, well-defined, static entities" with a conception of communities as "porous, multifaceted, ever-shifting, loosely connected groups of people" (2013, 81). Similarly, Linnell Secomb argues that insofar as identity is constituted in and through relations with others and thus is never autonomous, singular, unified, or static, but rather is relational, heterogenous, fractured, situated, and in process – it is, we might say, networked – then so too is community. Drawing on the work of French philosopher Jean-Luc Nancy (2000, 1991), Secomb proposes "an interpretation of community as an expression of difference and diversity that is made manifest through disagreement and disunity" (2000:134). This "queer/ing community" (1997), she claims, is disruptive of the logic of identity that Young critiques insofar as it engenders and is engendered by heterogeneity, by the transgression of boundaries, identities, categories. Community, in this sense, rather than denying or covering over differences in the service of unity, is the experience of the impossibility of communion, the experience of radical difference. Community is, as Secomb conceives it, “a being-together animated by resistance, discord, and disagreement” (2000:147): it is an unworking of the myth of oneness that allows for the recognition of irreconcilable but productive differences and the debates generated in and through these. Community, in this sense, is more like what Latour refers to as a gathering, an assembling of people, ideas, and things: it is something we do (a verb), rather than something we are (a noun). So what might this mean in terms of museological practice, and in particular, collaboration with external stakeholders?

The mechanics of collaboration

“The promise of unmitigated inclusion” (Robinson, cited in Haviland, 2017:889) that underpins the traditional understanding and practice of community engagement in museums, is, we argue, a contradiction in terms. Simply put, inclusion is inextricable from exclusion: in order for someone to claim an identity and/or membership of a particular group, someone else must be denied access, must “form the constitutive outside to the domain of the subject” (Butler, 1999:236). The extent to which the failure to recognise this can contribute to feelings of disappointment and frustration, to loss of trust, and to a reluctance to engage in collaborative projects should not be underestimated. A project in which there was no disagreement would be a project in which difference had been entirely negated, in which unity and/or consensus had been achieved through the (costly) imposition of a single, dominant frame. Even if this were possible – and we very much doubt that it is[9] – it is certainly not politically desirable. At the same time, there is no guarantee that discord and disagreement will engender productive debate and open up new ways of knowing, being, and doing, that it will not prove too uncomfortable, too risky, to difficult, and thus lead to the abandonment of ‘difficult’ projects in favour of less challenging ones. If we want to avoid, on the one hand, assuming that consensus equals success, and, on the other, romanticising incommensurability, how might we critically reflect on, evaluate, and revise collaborative processes and practices?

In order to critically engage with the ways in which different, situated gatherings or matters of concern are enacted, and thus produce different socio-political effects – to explore whether and how such gatherings queer heteronormative ways of knowing, being, doing – it is important to attend to what Maya Haviland refers to as the mechanics of collaboration. In order to explain Haviland’s claim we want to begin by suggesting that collaborations be understood as networks consisting not only of the parties involved – each with their own (complex and contradictory) identities, modes of action, idea(l)s, and the ethos that shapes them – but also, the diverse, and context-specific, opportunities and constraints associated with a given time, place, project. Every collaborative project involves “unique groupings of relationships, histories, political, economic and cultural moments" which act as "enabling and constraining factors" (2017:889), and as such, assessments of participatory practices must pay close attention to the specificity of the networked context, the multiple axes around which they occur. Of the many possible axes that might shape any given project, Haviland identifies three.

The first concerns the agency of participants and the extent of their collaboration in various aspects and/or stages of a project (Haviland, 2017:887). At one end of this axis is the conviction that the community members should play a role equal to that of museum staff in every aspect of a collaborative project (including its conception) and in every decision made. At the other end, external participants may simply be consulted regarding the accuracy of information about a particular object or issue that forms part of an exhibition. Rather than assuming that the former approach is preferable to the latter, as many proponents of community engagement as socially inclusive do, Haviland suggests that critically interrogating the mechanics of collaboration as they are enacted in a specific context may enable us to problematise such value hierarchies, and to acknowledge the importance of diverse approaches to collaboration and to the opening up of ways of knowing, doing, and being.

The second axis Haviland identifies is characterised by the privileging of high production values (tangible outcomes such as an on-time, highly professional looking exhibition) at one end, and process (skill development, trust-building, and other less quantifiable effects) at the other. Again, she eschews the idea that one of these is, by definition, more important than, or more in keeping with a social justice approach, than the other, and suggests instead that the position on the spectrum that is most appropriate can only be determined by the specificities of a particular project and the circumstances in which it occurs.[10] The third axis "maps those projects that prioritise object-based versus relational outcomes" (2017:888). What Haviland means by this is that some projects may form one step in an ongoing process of engagement, the outcomes of which only become visible and thus measurable over an extended duration. In cases such as this, a single exhibition may be interpreted by some as less than ideal because, for example, it provides a chronology of LGBT activism in a particular place, but does not ultimately queer heteronormative notions of community, identity, temporality, and so on. However, if the exhibition is part of an ongoing engagement with 'queerness' or with particular individuals, organisations, and issues, then evaluation needs to take a broader, more long-term focus.

What Haviland's examples of the mechanics of production draw attention to is the fact that

> real world collaborations are always multiply situated. [That] each is shaped by unique groupings of relationships, histories, political,

> economic and cultural moments. . . [and] span[s] divergent social change objectives, and different perceptions of value by [the]actors involved.
>
> (2017:889)

Unfortunately, the mechanics of production are rarely visible to those not intimately involved in a project: indeed, they are most often not understood in the same way by everyone who is involved.[11] Moreover, as we suggested earlier, the multiple, complex processes involved in the development and implementation of a project – whether it be a single exhibition or a series of collaborations of varying kinds – are rarely documented, reflected on, and made publicly available, and, consequently, it is extremely difficult to critically evaluate museological projects 'from the outside'. But as Haviland convincingly demonstrates in her response to Helen Robinson's (2017) critique of the National Museum of Australia's *Encounters* exhibition, critical evaluation that is unaware of internal processes, of the constraints faced, the debates had, the decisions made, and the reasons for making them, can be highly problematic.

Given this, we need to conceive collaborative projects, exhibition-making, and other museological undertakings as both products and generators of scholarships, that is as effects of specific, situated ways of knowing, doing, and being, and as opportunities to interrogate, and rework museological methodologies and their contributions to world-making. Envisaging practice as scholarship, as work that produces not just things (exhibitions, public programmes, and so on) but also, and no less importantly, methodologies, has a range of radical implications. First, it not only requires documentation and critical reflection, it locates these things at the heart of practice (rather than as something we might do on the rare occasion that we have some spare time). Second, it (re)connects the work that each of us does in our own situated contexts to a global network in which methodological approaches, insights, challenges, and so on are continuously de/re/constructed and configured *in-relation*; hence the need to make the critical documentation of practice available, accessible, and as transparent as possible. Third, this provides an opportunity to consider particular projects (or aspects thereof) as other than simply successes or failures,[12] and instead to conceive them as part of the ongoing (networked) process of developing, critiquing, and reconfiguring ways of knowing, doing, and being. Fourth, this approach allows for multiple interpretations of the same project, multiple perspectives that gesture towards the ways in which positionality comes to matter, and shows that ultimately consensus and/or community (as it is conventionally understood) is both impossible and politically and ethically undesirable. Fifth, it allows us to rethink difference, discomfort, contestation, and creative conflict, as productive (even if difficult and uncomfortable) opportunities, rather than simply difficulties to be overcome. In order to further elaborate these claims and the alternative conceptions of community offered earlier, we turn now to three quite different examples of collaborative practice.

OUT at the Museum: from matters of fact to matters of concern

One of the claims most commonly made in museological literature on inclusion is that museums can change lives by empowering individuals and communities; contribute to enhanced self-esteem, confidence, creativity, self-determination, and so on; promote understanding and respect; and challenge misconceptions, stereotypes, and prejudice.[13] These compelling idea(l)s, and the assumptions about community and identity that underpin them, shaped our invitation to attendees of Adelaide's Feast Queer Youth Drop-in (a space for 15- to 25-year-old queer-identified people) to mount an exhibition in the Migration Museum's[14] community access gallery (known as The Forum). They also shaped the approach we initially took.

The Forum gallery was established in the early 1980s as an inclusive space in which community groups could tell their stories in their own words, and display objects that might not ordinarily be deemed museum worthy; it was envisaged as a place that would enable visitors "to engage with, make sense of and negotiate difference, in ways which privilege concepts of equality, cross-cultural understanding and mutual respect" (Sandell, 2007a:72). A radical innovation when it was first established, the community access gallery has become something of a home-away-from-home for established ethnic groups in Adelaide, many of whom migrated to Australia in the second half of the twentieth century. Despite the assumption of a shared identity based on race and/or ethnicity, the groups who mount Forum exhibitions are never wholly representative of the communities they call their own. Indeed, some hold nostalgic and static views of their culture that have little in common with the views that others from the same geographic location may have of themselves and the place from whence they came.

While we value the important contributions these groups make, our decision to approach the Queer Youth Drop-in was, in part, motivated by a concern that despite the principles of diversity and access on which the community gallery was built, the space is typically dominated by small established groups with a strong sense of shared identity – what Phelan describes as ascriptive community – with more marginalised or less coherent groups (more often nonascriptive communities) typically rarely being represented.[15] This is not because the latter have approached the museum with suggestions for exhibitions that have been declined. It may be because they are unaware of the museum's existence, or do not connect with it, or because they do not identify as a community. Whatever the reason, an 'open door' approach to community access galleries fails to consider the ways in which heteronormative structures of identity, power, and privilege operate to include and exclude such that some groups are better placed to access the community gallery than others. Tendencies such as this speak volumes about the hierarchisation of particular ways of being, knowing, and doing, and the fact that museums, while tackling some forms of marginalisation, can inadvertently contribute to others. As Sandell has argued, museums reflect and reinforce social exclusion both "directly, by promoting and affirming the dominant values, and indirectly, by subordinating, rejecting [or simply failing to recognise and foster] alternate values" (Sandell, 1998:408), and, we might add, failing to critically interrogate heteronormative concepts such as 'community', the epistemological assumptions that subtend them, and the very real material effects they produce.

Our desire to create a "contact zone" (Clifford, 1997) where "new voices and visibilities are raised and new knowledge(s) actively constructed" (Golding, 2013:25), led us to invite a community leader and a long-term attendee of the Drop-in to co-facilitate the project, raise funds to cover production costs, work with attendees to collect objects and stories for display, and write panel content. Our aim in doing this was, vis-à-vis Haviland's second axis, to ensure high production quality and a professional outcome in order to satisfy institutionalised norms. Our next step was to visit the Drop-in and explain our plans to the young people. Disappointingly, they were less than enthusiastic, and we left feeling somewhat defeated and confused. This led us to critically reflect on our approach and the assumptions that informed it. We realised that before even meeting the Drop-in attendees we had identified them as a nonascriptive community: as young and queer-identified and thus, in some sense, as being the same, and having the same needs and desires.[16] We had assumed a common identity that we uncritically associated with marginalisation and voicelessness. From there we had surmised that the attendees desired to be heard, and that the community access gallery would provide an opportunity to achieve this that was too good to be missed.

Rather than recognising these assumptions as both our own, and as problematic, we took them to be matters of fact. Reflecting later on the limits of our thinking we realised that rather than simply offering Drop-in attendees a once-in-a-lifetime opportunity, we were asking them to give us, complete strangers, their time and energy, their stories, an exhibition, and we were doing so without first discussing with them what mattered to them, whether they felt the need to have their voices heard, and so on. Despite our best intentions we had, we realised, imposed a vision that was *ours*, on a group of people with whom we had no previous relationship. In short, our assumptions about the identity, needs, wants, and desires of this group had blinded us to the structural inequalities that underpinned our relationship with them resulting in *us* setting the agenda and inadvertently reproducing the processes of exclusion that we had initially set out to counter. Horrifying as it now seems to us, we had inadvertently employed what Lynch describes as the "rhetoric of service [that] places the subject [community] . . . in the role of 'supplicant' or 'beneficiary', and the giver [museum] . . . in the role of 'carer'" (2017:26). We had failed, albeit unintentionally, to recognise (amongst other things) the agency of the young people involved, the group's heterogeneity, and our own investment in particular ideal(s).

Reflecting on our initial approach, we decided instead to regularly attend the Drop-in meetings as participant-observers, to take much more of a back seat than we had initially imagined we would. We engaged an artist to run an art making workshop for attendees irrespective of whether or not they intended to participate or display their works in the exhibition, and this turned out to be a fruitful way for conversations to emerge organically. Thinking about social justice, activism, and matters of concern (and the fact that these are many, varied, and perhaps not as easily identifiable as we had assumed), we also took along a badge maker, a large selection of LGBTIQ+ badge designs, and a set of blank templates with us each time we visited the Drop-in. Badge making proved to be a great way to connect with (most of) the young people who were there each week, to strike up conversations, and to gain insights into the issues that really mattered to them. In Latourian terms, the badge maker engendered an assembling, it gathered together a diverse group of people, each with their own embodied histories, dispositions, and agendas; it generated different connections, emotions, opinions, and dis/agreements; and provided opportunities to exchange ideas about a range of matters of concern including identity, love, sex, the environment, feminism, marriage equality, unicorns, disability, families, food, activism, etc.

Rather than being wholly outcomes-focussed we learned (although not always easily and never wholly) to appreciate the process in all its richness, complexity, and uncertainty. Right up until the last minute we were unsure exactly what was going to be displayed in the exhibition, but we regularly regrouped and reminded ourselves of the social value of the work we were involved in, that, as Kinsley argues, "an exhibition. . . [is] as much about the process of building relationships with community members as about building an installation" (2016:475). Knowing that the community gallery is "a space that is coming under increasing pressure . . . from within the museum sector itself, with increasing professionalisation and what could be described as a risk averse culture driving a need for a more polished or professional presentation" (O'Reilly & Parish, 2015:298–299), we oftentimes felt caught between competing imperatives. We did our best to satisfy both, and repeatedly reminded one another that rather than trying to resolve the tension between collaborative process and institutional expectations regarding outcomes, we would work with what at times felt like incommensurable ways of knowing, doing, and being.

The experience of collaborating with the Queer Youth Drop-in attendees showed us that whilst loosening one's grip on the reins and being willing to moderate one's practice can be risky, it can also pay enormous dividends. We had a successful launch, an exhibition that the young people felt ownership of and pride in, and a gallery full of moving, interesting, and informative content that received extremely positive responses from diverse publics. We have an ongoing relationship with Drop-in staff and with many of the young people who contributed to *OUT at the Museum*. The collaboration provided an amazing opportunity for us to critically reflect on the structures of power and privilege that underpin and inform our relationships with collaborators, our approach to 'community engagement' (a term we are increasingly loathe to use), and the ways in which our work can challenge heteronormative ways of knowing, doing, and being and the injustices that attend them. It also clearly demonstrated to us that abstract ideals, such as the claim that all collaborators should be equally involved in all aspects of a given project at all times, are problematic, and ultimately tend to homogenise rather than to make space for different desires, dispositions, interests, and abilities. At no point in the project did any of the young people from the Drop-in show any interest in taking charge of the project. Indeed, whilst many ultimately participated in one way or another, only a very small proportion of them were involved in the installation of the exhibition, and none were interested in documentation processes or the design of promotional materials.[17]

Queering the centre

While *OUT at the Museum* began with problematic assumptions about the group with whom we collaborated, the Walker Art Gallery's (WAG) project *Coming Out*: *Sexuality, Gender, & Identity* acknowledged and foregrounded the heterogeneity of LGBT+ identities, groups, issues, and concerns from the outset, building this into the heart of the project. The exhibition, which marked the fiftieth anniversary of the *Sexual Offences Act 1967* that partially decriminalised sex acts between (some) men, in private, in England and Wales, included artworks which reflect "how our understanding of sexuality, gender and identity has changed" (Keenan McDonald, 2017:5) since that time. At the conceptual, symbolic, and literal centre of the exhibition was a "collaborative space between audience and institution, curation and engagement" (Keenan McDonald, 2017:25) that the curators called FORUM (Figures 4.1 and 4.2), and that, from our perspective, shifted the exhibition away from the logic of identity (and of the closet) that its title may appear to embrace.[18]

Charlotte Keenan McDonald and Angelica Vanasse embarked on this project with an awareness that their knowledge of LGBTIQ+ identities, lives, histories, issues, and so on, was incomplete, and that the Walker Gallery "has been part of the heteronormative, patriarchal and imperialist social order which has historically marginalised and oppressed LGBT+ and BAME (Black, Asian and Minority Ethnic) communities, amongst others" (2017:25). Rather than attempting to cover over the institution's history, their own situated and (necessarily) partial perspective, and/or the fact that the artworks included in the exhibition did not (and could not possibly) comprehensively address 'queerness' in all its heterogeneity, the curators consulted with a range of individuals and groups and developed a flexible, modular space that could be (re)arranged to support multiple and changing occurrences and outcomes which would "respond to or fill gaps" (2017:26) in the exhibition. FORUM was intentionally left empty for the first few

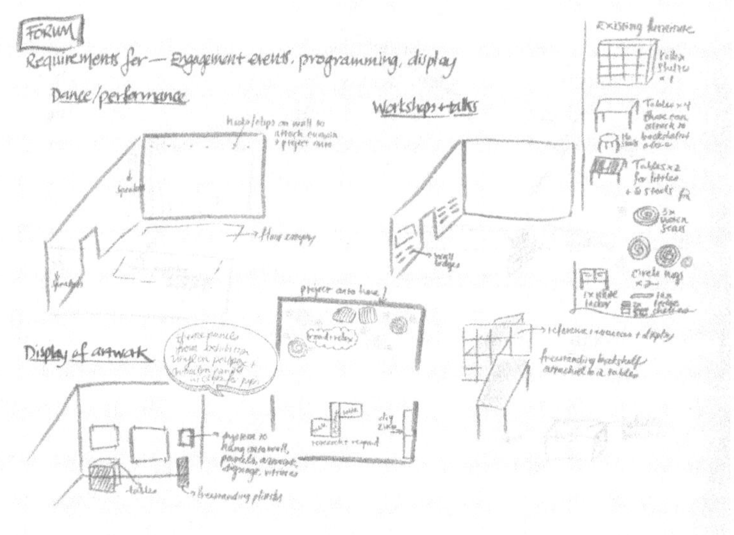

Figure 4.1 Sketches for FORUM, 2017

Credit: Courtesy Angelica Vanasse

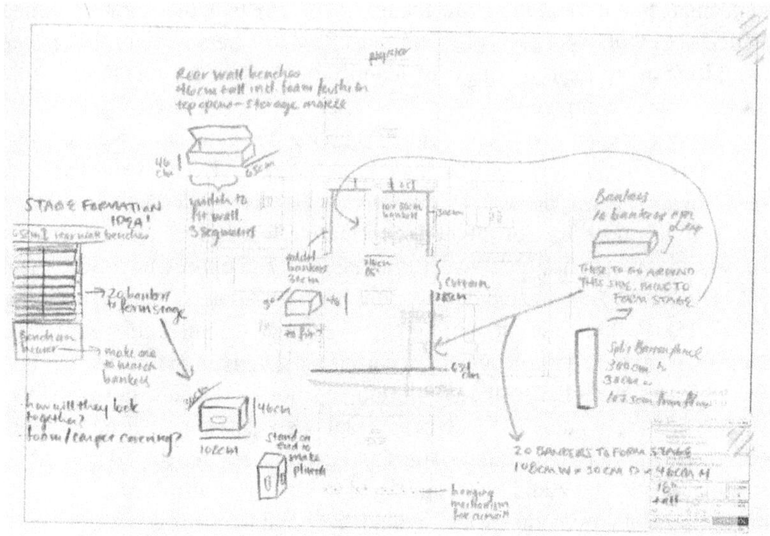

Figure 4.2 Sketches for FORUM, 2017

Credit: Courtesy Angelica Vanasse

weeks of the exhibition to symbolise the absence of LGBTIQ+ art and artists within art museums. The space was subsequently progressively populated with co-created content that queered homo- and heteronormative knowledges, practices, and identities. There was no attempt made by curators to make the changing content in FORUM cohere, to present a unified vision of community and consensus, or to incorporate it seamlessly into the rest of the exhibition. Indeed, Keenan McDonald argues that FORUM threw new and shifting light on the artworks that encircled it, furnishing visitors with alternative lenses through which to engage with the works. In so doing, FORUM reconfigured the artworks from what some may have taken as matters of fact (objects which have single meanings embedded in them by the artists who create them and made accessible by experts who objectively interpret them), to matters of concern, to active participants in the assembling of people and ideas, in the fabrication of networks and worlds. Likewise, the exhibition can also be understood as a process of contestation and negotiation, a practice and a space that not only welcomes "differences of opinion" (Lynch, 2017:34), but engenders and maintains their articulation.

FORUM featured a significant number of events, performances, and works, including John Walter's 'Alien Sex Club', which took a unique approach to the complexities of sex and sexual health, in particular the risk of the transmission of HIV/AIDS in the age of chemsex[19] (Keenan McDonald, 2017:60). The installation featured (amongst other colourful, provocative things) an inflatable, three-metre-high, neon 'Pug Virus',[20] and virus-bedecked tarot card reader Barbara Truvada,[21] both creations of Walter. Using the 78-piece deck of tarot cards designed by Walter, in which the four suits refer to the typologies of gay men's HIV risk stratification – 'the bugchasers, the giftgivers, the barebackers and the serosorters' – Truvada (aka Walter) at once exposed and challenged the myths and negative stereotypes surrounding HIV and its transmission. The cards, Walter claimed, made possible (what might otherwise be difficult and painful) conversations between Truvada and visitors around sexuality and cultural transmission. Similarly, in 'Nail Transphobia', transgender activist Charlie Craggs transformed FORUM into a pop-up nail salon in which visitors were offered free manicures while Craggs led critical conversations about transgender issues. As Craggs explains it, this ritual "gives us the chance to sit down and have a chat, they can ask me questions about being trans and I can teach them how to be an ally" (cited in Keenan McDonald, 2017:44). To us, these performances, and their positionality at the heart of *Coming Out*: *Sexuality, Gender, & Identity*, literally assemble people, ideas, and objects in order to facilitate discussion, debate, and learning around specific issues, or blind spots, both within and beyond the exhibition. In doing so, they enact what Joseph describes as "a critical relationship to community, as an ethical practice of community" (cited in Strickland, 2004:182). While *Coming Out*, as a collaborative project that engendered heterogenous (tangible and intangible) outcomes, and involved varying levels of participation, clearly spoke to, of, and from a wide range of (often complex and intersectional) positions and perspectives, it largely queered rather than reaffirmed inclusion discourse and the problematic assumptions about identity, community, and belonging that subtend it.

Te Ara Wairua: gathering, (re)activating, connecting, queering

Te Ara Wairua[22] was a collaborative project[23] that explored "multiple forms of digital materialities and engagements with [a Māori cloak] . . . and the discourses of the digital and the social that the project . . . brought together" (2018:89). It comprised a number of elements which could be understood as matters of fact: most particularly Māori and non-Māori collaborators (as members of separate and distinct ascriptive communities), the cloak (as object rather than agent), the digital surrogate (the 3D image as visual object), and 'the digital' (as a reified object). However, from our perspective,[24] *Te Ara Wairua* resisted – albeit at times inadvertently – the all too easy conflation of things with facts, with fixity, with the logic of identity, and in doing so queered widely held idea(l)s about community, identity, objects, meaning, provenance, and digitisation. At the heart of the project was a small Māori cloak woven from flax and decorated with tassels made from the hair of the Polynesian dog (*Kuri*).[25] The cloak had been transferred to University College London's (UCL) ethnography collection from the Wellcome collection in the 1940s and was catalogued as being of "unknown provenance" (Geismar, 2015:307). *Te Ara Wairua*'s aim was to (re)connect the cloak to living Māori people and knowledges, and "to reactivate the spiritual pathways, the *wairua*, that all Māori *taonga* [cultural treasures] instantiate" (2015:308) using a range of digital technologies including 3D imaging, real-time connection, and immersive light and sound installations.

The project began with the creation of a ceremonial space, a *marae*, in which collaborators from the UK and Aotearoa New Zealand gathered, via screen-based projections and cellular and broadband pathways and data flows, to stand before the cloak, speak in (and listen to) chants (*karakia*) and song (*waiata*), and share breath. This was followed some weeks later by another Facetime session which, like the first, was beset with technological difficulties.[26] In this second gathering the cloak was given the name *Tukutuku Roimata*, "the tears of the ancestors from the spiritual realm interwoven and connecting us with the physical realm through the Korowai" (as translated by Kura Puke) (Geismar, 2018:93). This name(ing) simultaneously articulates both the grief associated with the cloak's absence from a known *whakapapa* (or web[s] of relationships in which everyone and everything is situated), and the emergence of new networks of connection[27] as cause for celebration (2018:93). During the greeting that formed a central part of the gatherings the voices of the New Zealand–based participants were translated into colour gel lights that bathed the space in which the cloak was housed, and the voices of UCL participants passed through LEDs built into the cloak's case (Geismar, 2018:93) thereby warming her,[28] materialising the vital energy necessary for the articulation and maintenance of webs of connectivity. The collaboration thus shifted away from an initial focus on visual representation to an understanding of the gatherings (and the elements of their articulation) as "channels for social and spiritual relationships" (2015:313). Outside of the ceremonial gatherings, the same LED lights transmitted sounds of birdsong and Māori song to the cape, thereby (re)locating her, although never wholly or in any singular sense, within a Māori environment and cosmology,[29] and maintaining and reconfiguring both networked connections and the channels through which they are engendered.

At the same time, drawing on contemporary museological ideas about the potential of the digital to create experiences that are as good as, if not better than, encounters with the 'real thing', Geismar worked with technicians at UCL to create a 3D version of the cloak that "might facilitate access that transcended the limitations of the cloak's size and fragility" (2015:309) and conservation considerations which meant that the cloak could only be displayed flat (and not, as she was meant to be, worn) and could not be touched. Geismar initially assumed that it would be possible to produce a "flawlessly photographic" three-dimensional representation of the cloak (as it would appear on a body), which may, through the use of avatars and virtual reality, be able to be worn. What she learned was that far from simply capturing reality, digital surrogates are the composite effect of complex technological processes, creative decisions made by skilled practitioners, and the technical and conceptual worlds in which they operate.

Geismar also tells how the cloak resisted digitisation – in as much as both the woven flax and the dog hair tassels presented a range of problems for scanners – and, as a Māori treasure, demanded to be conceived beyond the logic of "the photographic lexicon" (2018:96), which cannot speak to or of the intangible character of objects, their agency, their role in the engendering of affect, or their networked character. In other words, *Te Ara Wairua* "instantiated a philosophy of connection" (Geismar, 2018:96), of networks, and in doing so, reconfigured the digital as affective rather than simply representational: *wairua*, writes Geismar, is

> both a synonym and an encompassing term for the digital. Just as the digital exists in waves of information, transmitted all around us, so too do *taonga* create networks of connectivity, across both space and time. The connection of this cloak, through broadband and cellular activity, to people in both London and New Zealand was therefore framed not as something new, but as a continuation of the kind of work that *taonga* are supposed to do – to link people, activate and maintain connections and networks of knowledge and sociality.
>
> (2018:90)

What Geismar initially saw as the failure of technology to bring communities into communion enabled a reconfiguration of the collaboration as other than unifying and redemptive, as, instead, an "attempt to recreate a connection that *can never be fully salvaged*, to work across a distance *that is still present*, to work across *interpretive gaps* in language, cosmology, within the interstices of colonial history" (2018:93, emphasis added).[30] At the same time, the impossibility[31] of determining the cloak's original makers and owners provided an opportunity to move beyond singular fixed notions of objecthood, truth, ownership, community, and so on, and to explore the ways in which Māori epistemologies and cosmologies, "improvised in new environments and using new tools" (2018:91), can "encircle those brought in through the process of settler-colonialism" (2018:89). Like *Tukutuku Roimata* – the tears of the ancestors that are engendered by, engender, and embrace the co-presence of multiple, contradictory registers of knowledge, meanings and affects, pasts, presents, and futures – *Te Ara Wairua*, and the cloak that animated it, assembled disparate bodies (of thought, of people, of institutions and cultures, of tangible and intangible heritage, of technology, of agency) and materialised "the energy of connection" (Puke, cited in Geismar, 2018:95) without attempting to reconcile differences or merge incommensurable elements into a unified whole. Through this process, Geismar and her colleagues were able to (re)conceive the cloak (both in its 'original' and its digital forms) as less an object that represents an ontology of networks, connections, co-presence, than "an active participant in its fabrication" (Geismar, 2015:316), and as itself, always already networked, heterogeneous, in-process. This (re)conception shares resonances with Latour's call for a shift from matters of fact to matters of concern. Moreover, the gathering and connecting that is affected in and through *Te Ara Wairua* offers us a way to think about community as other than unified, homogenous, clearly bounded, knowable, as, in short, subtended by and reproducing the logic of identity. Instead, what we see, feel, and are caught up in is an unpredicatable, affective, fractured, multifarious, open-ended coming together that queers the heteronormative epistemologies that subtend 'community engagement' as it is commonly understood and practised.[32]

Queer(ing) collaboration

All three projects discussed in this chapter differ with regard to their aims, audiences, and intentions, but for us, each, in different ways, these projects offer a performative articulation of collaboration that queers heteronormative ways of knowing, doing, and being. The first involved queering the common-sense notion of community, the assumptions that subtend it, and the effects it produces. The second at once mounted an exhibition around LGBTIQ+ identity, and troubled the logic of such by locating at its heart difference, complexity, absence, change, movement, flexibility, unknowing, and connectivity without communion. The third, *Te Ara Wairua*, explored knowing, doing, being as always already complex, connected, in-process, affective. Queer/ing collaboration, for us, acknowledges the complexity and limitations of its subject, community, and turns a critical eye to the processes of collaboration and the roles and positionalities of collaborators. In short, it performatively enacts queer ethics as discussed in Chapter 1.

Notes

1 Morse views community engagement as an extension of audience development, a practice designed to increase the size, breadth, and diversity of visitors to museums (Morse, 2018:172), primarily for financial reasons.
2 As Bernadette Lynch puts it, the "demand for public accountability, including involving their communities in more direct collaborations, has increased in museums in the light of global expectations for a greater degree of public participation and deliberation in civil society" (2011:441).
3 But despite this, museums and professional bodies continually attempt to define core principles and 'best-practice' around community engagement, often in the form of toolkits (Benetua et al., 2018; Museums Association, 2018; OMA, 2015), thereby implying that a one-size-fits-all model is both viable and desirable.
4 See, for example, Cobahee River Collective (1983), Ferguson (1984), Mohanty (1984), Haraway (1985), O'Sullivan (1997), Moreton-Robinson (2002), and Ahmed (2008). Debates about lesbian identity and its relation to feminism are explored also in *Go Fish* (1984) directed by Rose Troche, and in 1972, *If These Walls Could Talk 2*, (2000), directed by Jane Anderson, Martha Coolidge, and Anne Heche.
5 These group(ing)s may, in some cases, be more difficult for museums to identify. Consequently, collaboration with nonascriptive communities is often initiated by members of the groups rather than museum staff (although in some cases staff are themselves members of nonascriptive groups). For further discussion of the latter point, see Hollows (2019).
6 Here we are reminded of Zygmunt Bauman's claim that community is almost always represented nostalgically as either a 'paradise lost' – something we once had and wish to return to – or a 'paradise to be found' or made, that is, something which will exist in the future even though it may never have existed in the past (2000:1). While the critics of the *Lindow Man* exhibition discussed in the previous chapter bemoan a lost past (when experts were experts and that was that), or at least one that is under threat of extinction, inclusion discourse presupposes a future in which we will (or at least could) belong equally.
7 An example of this within a museum context is explored by Ealasaid Munro who, working with recent immigrants as part of a community engagement project with Glasgow Museums, explains the diverse makeup of the identified group whose "experiences varied widely" (Munro, 2014:48). Participants in this group had competing needs and considerations based on, for example, the extent to which their experiences of migration involved discrimination (Munro, 2014:48).
8 Later, in *Other Asias* (2008), Spivak rejects the term because of her dissatisfaction with the way in which it has been deployed in nationalist enterprises to promote (non-strategic) essentialism.
9 Michel Foucault claims that power is never absolute, that where there is power, there is always resistance. Indeed, one is the flipside of the other. See Foucault (1980), pp. 92–102. See also Heller (1996).
10 For discussion of a good example of a project that had very clear aims and objectives, and deployed specific conceptual frameworks, see Gibson and Kindon (2013).

11 An interesting example of this can be found in the very different accounts of *The Past is Now* offered by Wajid and Minott (2019) and Kassim (2017).
12 It is troubling to note the ubiquity of the seeming reluctance of practitioners and institutions to expose themselves to criticism, to acknowledge that an experiment or approach has not produced the hoped-for results, and to present over-inflated claims of success. This sort of disavowal works against critical self-reflection and change.
13 For example, Sandell (2003, 2007a, 2007b) and Fleming (2003).
14 South Australia does not have a Museum of South Australia's History and the Migration Museum operates as the primary state-run social history museum, which aims to engage with and share stories of all South Australians, and not only those who identify as having a conventional migration story.
15 This is in keeping with O'Reilly and Parish's claim that in community galleries less coherent, more marginalised groups are "not being represented at all" (2015:310).
16 The members of the Queer Youth Drop-in could have also been identified as an ascriptive community if sexuality and gender are understood as innate or 'natural'.
17 We are mindful, however, that the same project, involving a different group of participants, would inevitably be a different experience, and would require no less negotiation and critical self-reflection.
18 The centrality of FORUM to the exhibition demonstrated that engagement was integral to the projects rather than something that was added on in order to tick engagement boxes.
19 For more information, see Stuart (2019).
20 According to Ma, "Pug Virus is Walter's attempt to re-envision HIV in our current time of highly-effective antiretroviral therapy, a contrast to 1980s representations of the virus during the 'AIDS' crisis, tombstones and all" (2016:42).
21 Truvada is the name of a brand of Pre-Exposure Prophylaxis (PrEP), a drug which significantly reduces the risk of contracting HIV (up to 86%). Walter's use of Truvada highlighted a drug that, at the time of the exhibition, was little known amongst the wider public. It had only been recently funded by the NHS in the UK for a trial period of three years after a lengthy battle and a High Court ruling in favour of the National AIDS Trust, which had been fighting for the NHS to fund the drug.
22 *Te Ara Wairua* is a Māori phrase meaning "pathways of spiritual or intangible energy" (Geismar, 2018:88).
23 The project was a collaboration between Māori artist Kura Puke (who initiated the project), Haidy Geismar, a social anthropologist and Professor of Anthropology at University College London, interaction designer Stuart Foster from Massey University, Aotearoa New Zealand, and Te Matahiapo Research Organization based in Taranaki, Aotearoa New Zealand. Parts of the project also involved members of Ngāti Rānana, the London Maori Club, representatives of UCL Anthropology, Museums, and Collections, and other guests.
24 We are not suggesting that *Te Ara Wairua* was, in any essential sense, queer, or that everyone involved in the project interprets it in the way we do, or even in any shared way.
25 The Kuri is alleged to have become extinct around the time the Treaty of Waitangi, which gave birth to New Zealand, was signed.

26 During the ceremony the live video link faltered, and the London-based group were unable to hear all of the words of the chants spoken by elders in Pouakai. This "resulted in an experience of unequal reception" (Geismar, 2018:91) and a heightened anxiety about what effect this would have on the relationship between UCL and their collaborators in Aotearoa New Zealand. While Geismar initially saw the functionality of the technology as key to the project's success, collaborator Kura Puke felt that the "intention, or spirit, of the ritual was more important than the perfection of its form" (2018:92). This, and other differences between collaborators, which Geismar discusses, support Haviland's claim that "real world collaborations are always multiply situated. [That] each is shaped by unique groupings of relationships, histories, political, economic and cultural moments. . . [and] span[s] divergent social change objectives, and different perceptions of value by [the]actors involved" (2017:889).

27 These networks exceed (and therefore trouble) community as it is conventionally understood.

28 Geismar claims that "Māori cloaks are considered to be ancestral forms and are always women" (2015:307–308).

29 This has led to the creation of new protocols for the cloak's care. A set of lights and sockets has been left at UCL so that staff can plug the cloak into this immersive environment/connection while it is in storage. At the same time, people from Te Matahiapo "can dial into the cloak, bathing it with sound and channelling the digital sound frequency into light" (2015:314). In referring to this as a form of (re)connection with a Māori environment and cosmology, we are not suggesting that this should be understood as a simplistic return to a pure and unmediated past that is somehow wholly Māori, and that Māori is an essential, homogenous, autonomous, and unchanging entity. Rather, the (re)connections that are enacted in and through this project continuously cut across the boundaries that are integral to the logic of identity, and articulate the complexities of identity, meaning, objecthood, and so on as always already networked, and always in-process.

30 For us, *Te Ara Wairua* moves beyond the logic of cultural replication in which a nostalgic view of community as a 'paradise lost' demands that things be done as they always have been in order to enact a return, to reaffirm boundaries between us and them, past and present.

31 While it was not possible to make such determinations at the time *Te Ara Wairua* took place, the collaborators have not ruled out the possibility of doing so in the future.

32 For us, *Te Ara Wairua* is wonderfully illustrative of Bryony Onciul's concept of the 'engagement zone' as "unmapped, unpredictable, and inconsistent terrain that has the capacity to produce unexpected outcomes" (2013:85).

References

Ahmed, S. (2008). Some Preliminary Remarks on the Founding Gestures of the 'new materialism'. *The European Journal of Women's Studies*, 15(1), 23–39.

Baker, M., & Scheele, J. (2016). *Queer: A Graphic History*. London: Icon Books.

Bauman, Z. (2000). *Community: Seeking Safety in an Insecure World*. Oxford: Polity Press.

Benetua, L., Simon, N., & Garcia, S. (2018). *Community Issue Exhibition Toolkit*. Santa Cruz, CA: Santa Cruz Museum of Art and History. https://santacruzmah.imgix.net/uploads/Community-Issue-Exhibition-Toolkit-FINAL.pdf. Accessed January 5, 2019.

Butler, J. (1999). Bodies That Matter. In J. Proce & M. Shildrick (Eds.), *Feminist Theory and the Body: A Reader* (pp. 235–245). Edinburgh: Edinburgh University Press.

Clifford, J. (1997). *Routes: Travel and Translation in the Late Twentieth Century*. Cambridge: Harvard University Press.

Combahee River Collective. (1983). The Combahee River Collective Statement. In B. Smith (Ed.), *Home Girls: A Black Feminist Anthology* (pp. 272–282). New York: Kitchen Table/Women of Color.

Crooke, E. (2006). Museums and Community. In S. Macdonald (Ed.), *A Companion to Museum Studies* (pp. 170–185). Malden, MA, Oxford, UK, and Victoria, Australia: Blackwell Publishing Ltd.

Duncanson, I. (2005). Refugee Meanings. In A. Wagner, T. Summerfield, & F. S. B. Vanegas (Eds.), *Contemporary Issues of the Semiotics of Law* (pp. 19–34). Portland, OR: Hart Publishing.

Ferguson, A. (1984). Sex War: The Debate Between Radical and Libertarian Feminists. *Signs*, 10(1), 106–112.

Fleming, D. (2003). Positioning the Museum for Social Inclusion. In R. Sandell (Ed.), *Museums, Society, Inequality* (pp. 213–224). London: Routledge.

Foucault, M. (1980). *The History of Sexuality Volume 1: An Introduction*. New York: Vintage Books.

Geismar, H. (2018). *Museum Object Lessons for the Digital Age*. London: UCL Press.

Geismar, H. (2015). Post-Photographic Presences, or How to Wear a Digital Cloak. *Photographies*, 8(3), 305–321.

Gibson, S., & Kindon, S. (2013). The Mixing Room Project at Te Papa: Co-Curating the Museum with Refugee Background Youth in Aotearoa/New Zealand. *Tuhinga*, 24, 65–83.

Golding, V. (2013). Collaborative Museums: Curators, Communities, Collections. In V. Golding & W. Modest (Eds.), *Museums and Communities: Curators, Collections and Collaborations* (pp. 13–31). London: Bloomsbury.

Hall, C., & Kahaleole, L. (1993). Bitches in Solitude: Identity Politics and Lesbian Community. In A. Stein (Ed.), *Sisters, Sexperts, Queers: Beyond the Lesbian Nation* (pp. 218–229). New York: Penguin Books.

Haraway, D. (1985). A Manifesto for Cyborgs: Science, Technology and Socialist Feminism in the 1980s. *Socialist Review*, 80, 65–108.

Haviland, M. (2017). Encounters and the Axes of Collaboration. *International Journal of Heritage Studies*, 23(9), 886–890.

Heller, K. J. (1996). Power, Subjectification and Resistance in Foucault. *SubStance*, 25(1), 78–110.

Hollows, V. (2019). The Activist Role of Museum Staff. In R. R. Janes & R. Sandell (Eds.), *Museum Activism* (pp. 144–157). London: Routledge.

Kassim, S. (2017). The Museum Will Not Be Decolonised. *Media Diversified*. https://mediadiversified.org/2017/11/15/the-museum-will-not-be-decolonised. Accessed March 10, 2019.

Keenan McDonald, C. (2017). *Coming Out: Sexuality, Gender & Identity*. Liverpool, UK: National Museums Liverpool.

Kinsley, R. P. (2016). Inclusion in Museums: A Matter of Social Justice. *Museum Management and Curatorship*, 31(5), 474–490.

Lynch, B. (2017). The Gate in the Wall: Beyond Happiness-making in Museums. In B. Onciul, M. Stefano, & S. Hawke (Eds), *Engaging Heritage, Engaging Communities* (pp. 25–49). Woodbridge, Suffolk: The Boydell Press.

Lynch, B. (2011). Custom-Made Reflective Practice: Can Museums Realise Their Capabilities in Helping Others Realise Theirs? *Museum Management and Curatorship*, 26(5), 441–458.

Ma, R. (2016). *The Alien Sex Club*: A Cheeky Look at Contemporary Gay Culture and HIV. *British Journal of General Practice*, 66(642), 42.

Mohanty, C. T. (1984). Under Western Eyes: Feminist Scholarship and Colonial Discourses. *Boundary 2*, 12(3), 333–358.

Moreton-Robinson, A. (2002). *Talkin' Up to the White Woman: Indigenous Women and Feminism*. Brisbane: University of Queensland Press.

Morse, N. (2018). Patterns of Accountability: An Organizational Approach to Community Engagement in Museums. *Museum & Society*, 16(2), 171–186.

Museums Association. (2018). *Power to the People: A Framework for Participatory Practice in Museums*. UK: Museums Association. www.museumsassociation.org/download?id=1254507. Accessed January 5, 2019.

Nancy, J. L. (2000). *Being Singular Plural*, R. D. Richardson & A. E. O'Byrne (Trans.). Stanford: Stanford University Press.

Nancy, J. L. (1991). *The Inoperative Community*, P. Connor & L. Garbus (Trans.). Minneapolis: University of Minnesota Press.

Onciul, B. (2015). *Museums, Heritage and Indigenous Voice: Decolonising Engagement*. New York: Routledge.

Onciul, B. (2013). Engagement, Practice, Ethos. In V. Golding & W. Modest (Eds.), *Museums and Community* (pp. 79–87). London and New York: Bloomsbury.

Ontario Museums Association (OMA). (2015). *Engaging Your Community: A Toolkit for Museums*. Ontario, Canada: Ontario Museums Association. https://cdn2.hubspot.net/hubfs/316071/Resources/Tools/A%20CE%20Museums%20Engaging%20your%20Community%20Toolkit.pdf. Accessed January 5, 2019.

O'Reilly, C., & Parish, N. (2015). Telling Migrant Stories in Museums in Australia: Does the Community Gallery Still Have a Role to Play? *Museum Management and Curatorship*, 30(4), 296–313.

O'Sullivan, K. (1997). Dangerous Desire: Lesbianism as Sex or Politics. In J. J. Matthews (Ed.), *Sex in Public: Australian Sexual Cultures* (pp. 114–126). Sydney: Allen & Unwin.

Perkin, C. (2010). Beyond the Rhetoric: Negotiating the Politics and Realising the Potential of Community-Driven Heritage Engagement. *International Journal of Heritage Studies*, 16(1–2), 107–122.

Phelan, S. (1994). *Getting Specific: Postmodern Lesbian Politics*. Minneapolis: University of Minnesota Press.

Pishief, E. (2017). Engaging with Maori and Archaeologists: Heritage Theory and Practice in Aotearoa New Zealand. In B. Onciul, M. Stefano, & S. Hawke (Eds.), *Engaging Heritage, Engaging Communities* (pp. 83–104). Woodbridge, Suffolk: The Boydell Press.

Robinson, H. (2017). Is Cultural Democracy Possible in a Museum? Critical Reflections on Indigenous Engagement in the Development of the Exhibition Encounters: Revealing Stories of Aboriginal and Torres Strait Islander Objects from the British Museum. *International Journal of Heritage Studies*, 23(9), 860–874.

Sandell, R. (2007a). *Museums, Prejudice, and the Reframing of Difference*. Milton Park, Abingdon, OX and New York: Routledge.

Sandell, R. (2007b). Museums and the Combating of Social Inequality: Roles, Responsibilities, Resistance. In S. Wilson (Ed.), *Museums and their Communities* (pp. 95–113). London: Routledge.

Sandell, R. (1998). Museums as Agents of Social Inclusion. *Museum Management and Curatorship*, 17(4), 401–418.

Sandell, R. (2003). Social Inclusion, the Museum and the Dynamics of Sectoral Change. *Museum and Society*, 1(1), 45–62.

Secomb, L. (2000). Fractured Community. *Hypatia*, 15(2), 133–150.

Secomb, L. (1997). Queering Community. *Queerzone* (pp. 9–16). Nepean: University of Western Sydney Women's Research Centre.

Simon, N. (2016). *The Art of Relevance*. Santa Cruz, CA: Museum 2.0.

Spivak, G. C. (2008). *Other Asias*. Malden, MA: Blackwell Publishing.

Strickland, D. (2004). Beyond the Romance of Multiculturalism: Radicalizing Difference and Community in Cultural Studies. *College Literature*, 31(4), 181–187.

Stuart, D. (2019). Chemsex: origins of the word, a history of the phenomenon and a respect to the culture. *Drugs and Alcohol Today*, 19(1), 3–10.

Sullivan, N. (2003). *A Critical Introduction to Queer Theory*. New York: New York University Press.

Wajid, S., & Minott, R. (2019). Detoxing and Decolonizing Museums. In R. R. Janes & R. Sandell (Eds.), *Museum Activism* (pp. 73–86). London: Routledge.

Young, I. M. (1986). The Ideal of Community and the Politics of Difference. *Social Theory and Practice*, 12(1), 1–26.

Conclusion

Queering the Museum, as we stated in our Introduction, is underpinned by and builds on three claims that are commonly found in contemporary museological literature. In conclusion, we want to return to those claims and offer a brief summary of how the analyses we offer throughout the book have explored and substantiated them, and to what ends. The first claim is that museums are both shaped by and shape the socio-political landscapes in which they operate and are thus implicated in systems of power and privilege. In other words, far from simply offering neutral and objective 'facts' about a world that pre-exists its telling, museums offer situated, subjective, and necessarily partial narratives that contribute to world-making. They do this through, amongst other things, the kinds of practices of display discussed in Chapter 2, through cataloguing and collections development and management as discussed in Chapter 3, and through the ways in which they understand and engage with communities and other collaborators, which we explored in Chapter 4.

What our analysis of 'Truth Trophy' showed, for example, is that what is not displayed in museums is no less significant than what is: the absence of some people, histories, and interpretations constructs norms, idea(l)s, identities, values, relations of power, and worlds just as surely as does the (often ubiquitous) presence of others. And it does so, for the most part, without many of us noticing. Indeed, we have argued that we are all complicit in the reproduction of some norms and the inequalities they engender and hold in place, and this is because, as Bourdieu's account of habitus explains, the internalisation and reproduction of inherited ways of knowing, doing, and being, is, by and large, un-, or less-than-conscious. As a consequence, museum professionals are more likely to collect some things than others, to interpret, classify, and catalogue objects according to familiar (and thus comprehensible) paradigms, and, as Foucault's discussion of the literally fabulous taxonomy from an ancient Chinese encylopaedia shows, to never even imagine the unimaginable, to think what it is impossible to think. If we continue to operate uncritically within these known parameters of practice, we run the risk of never seeing beyond what we 'think' we know. As 'Truth Trophy' poignantly demonstrates, the introduction of excluded knowledges, people, and practices (potentially) troubles the naturalised, the taken-for-granted, the habituated. Wilson's work achieves this, we contend, not by replacing an erroneous, subjective, account of history with a true, objective one, but rather, by queering the notion of absolute truth, foregrounding it as an effect of what Foucault calls power/knowledge. At the same time his interventions illustrate the role that heterornormative, colonialist truth-effects have played (and continue to play) in the maintenance of structural forms of privilege and bias.

The second claim that subtends *Queering the Museum* is that, despite growing sectoral concerns around inclusion, LGBTIQ+ his/stories, lives, identities, and issues continue to be largely absent in museums internationally, and this has very real material effects. As we have shown, there are various possible responses to this situation, the most common of which is to call for inclusion, for an increased presence of LGBTIQ+ lives, histories, experiences, issues, works, and objects in museums. While acknowledging the import of inclusion discourse and practice, we have problematised some of the assumptions that inform such an approach. In particular, we ask what an LGBTIQ+ object is, what makes it LGBTIQ+ (or not), why and how. Tied to this is the question of the political and ethical (un)desirability of assuming that identity (whether of objects or people) is somehow innate, singular, autonomous, and knowable, rather than constructed, contingent, relational, intersectional, and always in-process. The effect of the former, we have suggested, is to further engender identity and difference in binary terms, to reproduce exclusion rather than to challenge the logic that produces it. Despite this, we are mindful that strategic essentialism is both necessary and effective in a range of ways and for a variety of reasons.

It is not our intention, then, to imply that queering is antithetical and/or inherently superior to inclusion, that the former is wholly distinct from that latter, or that any intervention could be 'purely' queer in its practice and effects. That the notion of inclusion "is questionable does not mean that we ought not to use it, but neither does the necessity to use it mean that we ought not perpetually to interrogate the exclusions by which it proceeds" (Butler, 1993:222). Indeed, this sort of 'perpetual interrogation from within' is precisely the work of queering. Integral to queering, then, is the recognition that since the work we (that is, museums and museum professionals) carry out is always multiply situated and contingent on contextually specific constraints and affordances, our activist arsenal must necessarily include a range of (sometimes seemingly contradictory) tactics: in one context we, and those with whom we collaborate, may choose (for a variety of reasons) to deploy 'truth-telling' as a strategy aimed at redressing the structural inequalities, past abuses, and ongoing material effects of colonialism, whereas in another we may, as in the case of *Lindow Man: A Bog Body Mystery*, be more concerned with foregrounding multiple interpretations that resist notions of truth.

In Chapter 4 we argued that decisions regarding exhibitions, public programmes, community engagement projects, or even hiring, are always shaped by the (institutional, socio-political, economic, historical, glocal) contexts in which they occur, and, as Bourdieu would argue, by the embodied dispositions of those making them. Given that these structured and structuring factors are often far from transparent – event to those involved – the evaluation of specific projects from the outside and/or on the basis of abstract criteria can be highly problematic, as our discussion of Haviland's account of the mechanics of collaboration has shown. Recognition of this has impacted the approach we have taken in the book in two ways. First, we have tried to avoid the god trick of proclaiming, as if from nowhere, the queerness (or otherwise) of specific exhibitions, approaches to collaboration, or documenting practices and processes. Instead we have focussed on elements of work with which we are familiar and which, to us, appear to potentially contribute to the queering of particular knowledges, practices, and structural inequalities. The claims we make about them are situated and partial but, we hope, nevertheless useful. Second, throughout the book we have attempted to move away from the rather narrow notion of the museum as an institution that houses collections and instead to rethink 'it' as a method, a heterogeneous and situated set of activities: a verb as much as a noun, As such we have called on museum practitioners to engage with museological scholarship, to understand the diverse forms of work we perform on a daily basis as praxis (as scholarship, as political and as world-making), and to document practice in critically informed and self-reflexive ways. If, as Martha Fleming argues, "it is methodologies that are the scholarly product of research, as much as the actual . . . shows produced" (2010:36), then it is crucial that we disseminate these critical accounts of how we make meaning, challenge (or not) museological conventions, reconfigure (or not) power relations in the institution, in what contexts, and to what ends, as widely as possible.

The third claim with which we began was that museums can, and should, be active participants in the articulation of critically engaged and socially transformative ways of knowing, being, doing. Throughout *Queering the Museum* we have critiqued the "myth of neutrality" (Janes & Sandell, 2019:41) and argued that museological practice is always political, and cannot be otherwise since it produces real-world effects. Moreover, we have suggested that museums have been, and continue to be, thoroughly complicit in the (re)production of ableist, colonialist, classist, racist, homo- and transphobic idea(l)s and the inequitable power relations with which they are associated. Our response to these ongoing, habituated, and normalised tendencies has been to offer an account of queering (or of queer curatorial practice) that involves critically analysing habituated knowledges, practices, and identities in an attempt to move beyond them. Queer/ing practice, can, as we have shown, take many forms, and involve all aspects of museum business: juxtaposing disparate objects; tracing object biographies; cataloguing diverse interpretations and multiple ontologies and making them publicly available; facilitating the emergence of previously marginalised voices, knowledges, and forms of engagement; and acknowledging the structural violence(s) caused by the idea that 'always and everywhere has it been this way' all (potentially) contribute to queering museums. Moreover, queering, as we have articulated it throughout the book, can, we argue, be thought of as the work of ethics and thus as an appropriate response to "the immorality of inaction" (2019:38) that Janes and Sandell convincingly argue is all too prevalent both in museums and in public life more generally. Countering heteronormativity is undoubtedly a complex, often uncomfortable, and ongoing challenge, that requires us to turn a critical eye on ourselves as much as on the institutions to which we belong. It is our hope that *Queering the Museum* will provide useful tools and insights for those already involved in museum activism, and inspire those who are not yet engaged. Join us and let's see how much of a difference we can make.

References

Butler, J. (1993). *Bodies that Matter: On the Discursive Limits of 'Sex'*. New York: Routledge.

Fleming, M. (2010). Thinking Through Objects. In S. Lehmann-Brauns & C. Sichau Helmuth Trischler (Eds.), *The Exhibition as Product and Generator of Scholarship* (pp. 33–47). Germany: Max Plank Institute for the History of Science.

Janes, R. R., & Sandell, R. (2019). Posterity Has Arrived: The Necessary Emergence of Museum Activism. In R. R. Janes & R. Sandell (Eds.), *Museum Activism* (pp. 35–53). London: Routledge.

Index

For Product Safety Concerns and Information please contact our EU
representative GPSR@taylorandfrancis.com
Taylor & Francis Verlag GmbH, Kaufingerstraße 24, 80331 München, Germany

www.ingramcontent.com/pod-product-compliance
Lightning Source LLC
LaVergne TN
LVHW010933110826
845149LV00013B/2573